THE ESSENTIAL
Triathlete

THE ESSENTIAL
Triathlete

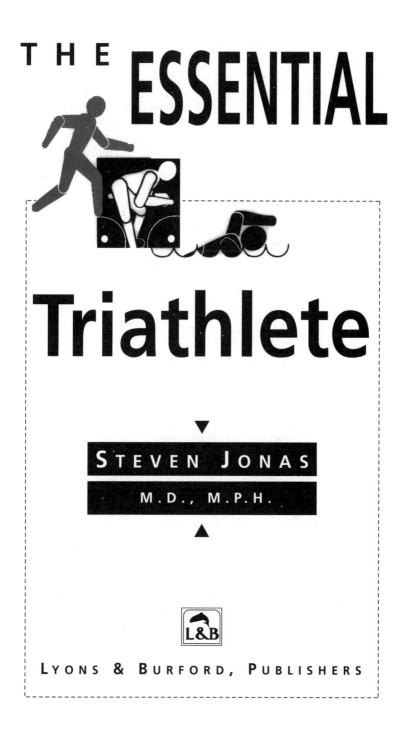

▼

STEVEN JONAS

M.D., M.P.H.

▲

L&B

LYONS & BURFORD, PUBLISHERS

Printed in the United States of America

Illustrations by Mitchell Heinze

10 9 8 7 6 5 4 3 2 1

Interior Design by: Howard P. Johnson
            Communigrafix, Inc.

Library of Congress Cataloging-in-Publication Data

Jonas, Steven.
    The essential triathlete / Steven Jonas.
        p.   cm.
    Includes bibliographical references and index.
    ISBN 1-55821-426-7
    1. Triathlon—Training—Handbooks, manuals, etc.
    I. Title.
    GV1060.73.J65   1996
    796.4'07—dc20   96-786
                                                CIP

This book is not intended to be a substitute for medical advice.
Anyone beginning a running program should receive clearance
from their doctor, especially those who are over 45 years old,
have a family history of coronary artery disease, or have any of
the other risk factors commonly associated with coronary artery
disease, such as high blood pressure, high cholesterol levels,
diabetes, obesity, or cigarette smoking.

CONTENTS

ACKNOWLEDGMENTS

First I thank Fred Feller, president of Carl Hart Bicycles of Middle Island, New York, and founder of Team Carl Hart, for all the help, encouragement, material benefit, and, most importantly, the friendship he has given me over the years.

I thank also Dan Honig, president of the New York Triathlon Club of Mt. Marion, New York, a stalwart of multisport racing almost since its inception, for his friendship and support since my early days as a tri- and duathlete. I would like to recognize the very significant contributions made to the sport in its early years by my friend Ray Charron, now of Kauai, Hawaii, as well as the encouragement and opportunity he gave me as a writer about triathlon. Many thanks to Lew Kidder, editor and publisher of *Triathlon Today!*, who gave me the opportunity to write regularly about the sport. Thanks to Chris Newbound, editor of *Inside Triathlon*, for his assistance. Thanks to Eric Swenson, my former editor at W. W. Norton, who gave me the opportunity to publish my first book on the sport. And thanks of course to my good friend John Hanc, who pioneered the "Essential" series for Lyons & Burford and made that first essential connection for me with the publisher, and to Lilly Golden, my editor at Lyons & Burford, who helped so much to put the book into its final form.

I would also like to thank Jim Borzell, Jane Gindin, Erika Hooker, Betsy Murphy, Charlie Ogilvie, Mark Sisson, and Andrew Tillin for their help and good cheer along the way.

Finally, many thanks to Steve Locke, executive director of the USA Triathlon, for honoring me, Lyons & Burford, and our book with their imprimatur.

Certain sections of this book are based in part on material I prepared for *Regular Exercise: A Handbook for Clinical Practice* (New York: Springer Publishing Co., 1995). It is used with the permission of the publisher.

Permission to use material of mine previously published in *Triathlon Today!* has been granted by the owner of the rights to *Triathlon Today!*, *Inside Triathlon* magazine. Permission to use material of mine previously published in *Triathlon Times* has been granted by its publisher, the USA Triathlon.

FOREWORD

*T*riathlon is a wide open sport. You don't need to be a highly trained athlete to get involved and reap the benefits.

I had been involved in sports all my life but had never considered triathlon until a friend invited me to watch him compete in one. I told him he was crazy. He replied, "This sport is right up your alley!"

Watching the triathlon, I was amazed to see that people were actually having *fun*. Up until that time, fun for me was going to an amusement park or simply sitting back with friends, sharing stories over beers. But a triathlon takes determination—you must set goals for yourself. I was so impressed that I bought a bike the very next day, rummaged around to find a schedule of future races, and decided to race two weeks later.

My two-week crash training course began immediately. I hadn't ever swum before and had never ridden a bike for any distance. My friend (knowing what he had gotten me into) was nice enough to give me some important training tips such as: "*don't drown*" and "*practice doing laps.*" I was being thrown—literally—into the deep end. But by the time I completed the race I was hooked.

After that first race, I was always on the lookout for the next race. I worked in construction six days a week saving travel money to attend races. After a few short triathlons, I wanted a bigger challenge, so I set my sights on the sport's ultimate challenge—the Ironman in Hawaii. I qualified for Hawaii in my second triathlon year and traveled to Kona not really knowing what to expect, but fulfilling the dream of a lifetime—to compete in the Ironman Hawaii Triathlon.

As triathletes, we are always looking for more ideas about how to improve performance. We want *all* the short cuts to better training, better nutrition, better racing. *The Essential Triathlete* is the complete package. It addresses all triathlon issues, from training to racing, from mental focus to resting—all extremely important in achieving maximum performance. Steve Jonas has gone to great lengths to explain each subject in simple and understandable detail. This book not only provides you with an exceptional way to get a head start on your triathlon competition, it also offers a few secrets to full enjoyment of the sport.

My experience with triathlon proves that dreams really can come true—that is, if you get your running shoes on the right feet in the transition area!

—Greg Welch, Winner, 1994 Ironman winner
Triathlon World Championship
Spring 1996

PREFACE

*T*hinking about doing your first triathlon? The event looks like it could be fun to do, three different sports and all that. Finishing one would be quite an achievement, wouldn't it? It would make you feel great, and as for telling friends, family, and coworkers about your accomplishment, well . . .

But you're a bit worried. You've heard that it's really tough to train for triathlon racing, that it takes a lot of time, effort, and energy, and that the races are always very challenging. It's true that *some* triathletes train a great deal and *some* races are *very* challenging. But *many* triathletes lead normal lives and train no more than five to six hours per week, total, for all three sports. That's the equivalent of running 30 to 35 miles per week, though your time is divided among running (or walking), cycling, and swimming. *Most* of the races are over reasonable distances on courses that do not present any special topographical difficulties.

Thus, while doing a triathlon race is both a mental and a physical challenge for anyone who tries it, it's not nearly as tough a nut to crack as many non-triathletes think it is. Most triathlons are not of the "gruelathon" variety as presented on television, and most triathletes do not do the sport in order to punish themselves.

Most triathletes are in the sport simply to have a good time, and most of us do so on most occasions. To have that good time does require a certain amount of physical work. But like most sports, triathlon has a major mental component as well the physical one. The focus of this book will be on meeting the mental challenge as well as the physical one.

Furthermore, the book reflects my thirteen years of experience in triathlon racing as a participant, not a competitor; as a "back-of-the-packer," not a pacesetter; as one who usually finishes but almost never wins a first-, second-, or third-place medal, unless there's only one, two, or three people in my age group. *The Essential Triathlete* is intended to be a concise and user-friendly guide to the most exciting and glamorous multiendurance-sport activity in the world, for the beginner, the novice, and the long-term recreational triathlete (and duathlete).

WHAT THE BOOK COVERS

*T*his book provides information on all aspects of multisport racing that involves swimming, cycling, and running. It will explore the mental and physical aspects of triathlon, and duathlon as well, and explain how you go about finding the races, and how to undertake an efficient, effective, and manageable training program. It will discuss technique, equipment, and, finally, actual participation in a race.

The book will show you how the ordinary recreational cyclist, runner, PaceWalker (also known as speed or fitness walker), or swimmer, even one who has never raced in any sport—or even someone who is not now an athlete—can become a triathlete in three to six months (the latter if you're starting from scratch).

The book will cover the broad spectrum of triathlon distances, including the **Sprint,** in the range of a ½-mile swim, a 15-mile bike, and a 4-mile run; the **Standard***, a 1.5k (0.93-mile) swim, a 40k (24.8-mile) bike, and a

---

*From about 1990 to 1995, this distance, which for years has been the most common one for triathlons, was called the "Olympic." After the sport gained official Olympic status in 1995, the International Olympic Committee asked the International Triathlon Union (ITU), the governing body for the sport, to drop the "Olympic" appellation. As of late 1995, no term other than the generic "triathlon" had been substituted for it, officially.

But to many recreational triathletes around the world, racing at many different distances, that may be confusing. It may well be that many race directors who have no direct or indirect connection to the ITU will continue to use the name "Olympic," just as many continue to use the word "biathlon" to describe two-sport events when again, for reasons of Olympic Committee relationships, the official term was changed several years ago to "duathlon." Not wanting to get in the middle of any controversies, but nevertheless wanting to clearly distinguish the distance for the purposes of this book, I've chosen to use the name "Standard" or "Standard-distance" for the 1.5k-swim/40k-bike/10k-run race.

10k (6.2-mile) run; and the **ironman,** a 2.4-mile swim, a 112-mile bike, and then, assuming you're still standing up, a 26.2-mile run. This book will *not* cover the double and triple ironman distances, for which, believe it or not, there are races—and racers.

Most triathlons are of the first two classes. This book should give you the guidance you need to finish your first triathlon happily, without injury, and without causing you to turn the rest of your life upside down. Presumably your first race will be of the Sprint or Standard variety, although I have known at least one person who for his first triathlon did an ironman-distance event.

YOUR BASIC REQUIREMENTS

*I*f you can swim in a reasonably straight line, keep your bike upright, and put one foot in front of the other on the run, you can do a triathlon. In fact, you don't have to be a special athlete, or even an athlete at all right now in order to participate. You don't have to be fast, either. If you can swim a mile in 45 minutes, bike 25 miles in 2 hours, and run a 10k in 65 minutes, you can do a Standard-distance triathlon in around 4 hours, and the average Sprint-distance event in 2 hours or less.

Those times are not unrealistically low, and if you come in under them you'll almost surely not be last. It does help to have some racing experience in one or more of the triathlon sports, but it's not essential. For many triathletes, their first triathlon has been their first race of any kind.

WHY TRY THE TRI?

*T*riathlon training is a great way to get and stay fit, healthy, and looking and feeling your best. The cross-training that you do—that is, working out in two or more sports at the same time—helps you to develop more than one major muscle group at a time, while most of the single sports focus on just one. Cross-training also reduces the risk of injury in any one of the sports, simply because you're doing less distance in each one. And the total time you spend working out builds up your general conditioning and endurance, regardless of which sport(s) you're spending most of your time on.

However, most of us who do triathlons do them simply because the training and the racing make us feel good and feel good about ourselves. Crossing the finish line is a thrill in itself. That feeling is what keeps many triathletes coming back for more.

THE TRAINING PROGRAM

*T*he *Essential Triathlete Training Program* (ETTP) (see chapter 3) is set in thirteen-week modules. There are four variants: the "Foundation," the "Standard-distance," the "Ironman-distance," and the "Maintenance" (for maintaining your conditioning in the off-season) programs. If you're already in "reasonably good aerobic shape" (as defined in chapter 3), you should be able to do your first triathlon at the Sprint or Standard length at the end of the thirteen-week Standard-distance training program.

If you're not already in "reasonably good aerobic shape," but are spending some time working out on a regular or even an irregular basis, in thirteen weeks the Foundation program should get you to the point at which you can comfortably start the Standard-distance program. All the programs are laid out in minutes, not miles. The primary objectives are to build up your physical and mental endurance. That done, you'll be able to be out on the course for the 2 to 4 hours it will take the slower triathlete to finish a Sprint or Standard-distance race.

Obviously, the faster your training paces, the more miles you'll cover in your training and the faster you'll be able to run, bike, and swim in the race. But it's the time spent, with consistency and regularity, not the distance covered, that's the key to success with this training program. If you train at reasonable paces for a reasonable amount of time, given the way the program is calculated and laid out, in all likelihood in that first race you'll be able to achieve your primary goal of finishing happily and without injury.

And that's all there is to it. You don't have to turn your life upside down. You don't have to work out endlessly. In fact, if you're already a regular exerciser, you'll probably find that on the average you're already spending close to the amount of time required by the Standard-distance program. You'll just be distributing that time differently.

PROLOGUE

On a bright and sunny Saturday in the fall of 1985, I was riding my bike north on Route 6, on Cape Cod, Massachusetts. I was somewhere between North Eastham and South Wellfleet, making my way north toward Provincetown. It was about noontime, and I was beginning to feel a bit hungry. Spying a fast-food place, I left the road, parked my bike safely, went inside, ordered a hamburger and a Coke (no fries), and proceeded to thoroughly enjoy the meal, even though I ate somewhat quickly.

A nice story, you might say, but certainly nothing unusual. True, riding a bike on Cape Cod and stopping for lunch are not unusual events, but doing the latter during the bike leg of an ironman triathlon (2.4-mile swim, 112-mile bike, 26.2-mile run) is a bit out of the ordinary, I believe. And, as I've told this story from time to time, I've come to feel that it encapsulates my attitude about the sport of triathlon racing.

I am not fast. In fact, I've always been rather slow, and as I get older, I'm getting slower, even though I stay in shape. But I love the sport and will be starting my fourteenth season in it, barring illness or injury, when this book is published. I go out there to do it, not to win it. I go out there to finish—in my own time: however fast or slow I go that day. I go out there to have a good time, to have fun, and I generally do. And that's what this book is about: having fun in the sport of triathlon racing.

And so, there I was, biking away on Cape Cod, doing my first ironman-distance triathlon (see chapter 8 for more on ironmanning). I had set up a schedule for myself for the race. I was slightly ahead of it. During a long training ride preparing for the race I had already tried out stopping in the midst of a long ride for a burger and a Coke, had suffered no ill effects, and had rather enjoyed the brief meal. On this day, I had the time, I had the hunger, and I finished my lunch. Much later that evening I finished the race, too.

IN THE BEGINNING

*M*y participation as an unlikely triathlete began in Cobo Hall, Detroit, in 1980. I was attending the Annual Meetings of the American Public Health Association and the Association of Teachers of Preventive Medicine (ATPM). At about 8:15 on the morning of Tuesday, October 21, I was walking up one of the ramps that connect the floors in that building on my way to do a workshop on "promoting legislative programs" (otherwise known as lobbying) with my good friend Dennis Barbour, then executive director of the ATPM.

I was breathless when I got to the top of that one-flight ramp. That was not a new experience. What followed was. I decided to do something about it. I decided to try, at least, to get into some sort of decent physical condition. For the first time in my life, I really wanted not to be out of breath after walking up a relatively short incline. The "learning moment" had occurred.

It's strange how these things happen. I happen to be a physician in the specialty of preventive medicine. At about that time, I happened to be doing some consulting work in prevention and medical education for the Texas College of Osteopathic Medicine in Fort Worth. That school had a very health-conscious faculty, at least one-third of whom exercised on a regular basis.

I knew all the scientific facts available at the time about the positive aspects of regular exercise, and knew how doing it would benefit my health. I had professional reasons to get with the program, too: As a consultant on prevention, shouldn't I be "showing the flag," as it were? But it was not those external motivators that got me going. It had to be something that came from the inside. I was stimulated neither by my knowledge nor by professional necessity, but rather by my own breathlessness. That's what made me recognize that I had to do something about my condition, for me, not for anyone else.

And so, at the beginning of November 1980, about three weeks before my forty-fourth birthday, previously a nonathlete (except for the highly technical and nonaerobic sports of downhill skiing and sailing), I took my first steps to becoming a regular aerobic exerciser (see chapter 3 for the definition of "aerobic").

I didn't know it then, but I had taken the first steps on a journey that would lead me to places I was at best only vaguely aware of at the time. I could not previously have even imagined myself wanting to get to them, much less actually reaching them. The vistas opened gradually, as I proceeded. Most wondrous of all, fifteen years later it's a journey I'm still on.

EXPLORING MY LIMITS

I began to explore my limits. I found out that they were not what I had thought they would be. First, I took up running, on the local high school track. I thought that I'd hate it, but it was the most time-efficient physical-conditioning sport that I knew of, and at my level (now as well as then) it takes no particular skill to do it. Within a short time I found, oddly enough, that not only did I not hate it; I actually liked it.

It took me a month before I could run a mile without stopping. Discarding the old pair of sneakers I had been using to get started (something I don't recommend now; see chapter 6), I went out and bought my first pair of running shoes. I started going for longer distances. I got off the track. I'll never forget the thrill I experienced the first time I ran up the hill out of our village of Port Jefferson, New York (which is located at the bottom of a topographical bowl, on one of the most beautiful harbors on the Long Island Sound). It was a clear day. I was beginning to be able to see forever.

During the summer season of 1981, I ran four to five times a week, 3 to 4 miles at a time. I was having a good time. Friends would ask if I had thought about racing.

"Not interested," I'd reply. Little did I know.

That fall, starting to get a bit bored with just running, I went out and bought my first ten-speed bike, yes my first bike of that type, ever. As a child in New York City, I had had a Schwinn with the double horizontal top bars and the horn-holder case mounted between them. And then when I was a teenager my mother had brought me a bike from England, a gleaming black Raleigh "English bike" with a four-speed shifter. Heaven! But I had never progressed to a "ten-speed." Now I did. I found that I liked the variety introduced by adding cycling to running. And that winter I actually found myself doing a bit of weight lifting at a local gym. For the first time in my life, I was actually becoming an *athlete*.

MY FIRST RACE

*B*y the next spring, for reasons that have never been clear to me, I entered my first race. On Memorial Day 1982, encouraged by my old friend Charles Arnold, M.D., I finished my first running road-race, a 5-miler on the rolling hills of the village of Belle Terre, New York, right outside of Port Jefferson. Chuck pulled me gently along until at about mile 4 he took off, knowing that I'd finish the race. I ran that race considerably faster than I thought I could at the time (at about an 8.5-minutes-per-mile pace considerably faster, as it happens, than I could do now).

Nevertheless, I recognized my limitations. Compared to the most of the runners out there, I wasn't fast at all. Given my body build, and my innate slow-footedness, it was unlikely that I ever would be fast. So I didn't worry about fast. However, I already knew that I hadn't come close to finding the limits of my endurance. Maybe, just maybe, I could go quite a way, slowly.

I set my next goal, to do a 10k (6.2-mile) road race. When I completed my first one, later that summer of 1982, I broke down and cried. With a few more road races under my belt by the end of that season, I had, in my own mind at least, become a racer. [And I had become a runner, too, rather than a jogger. After all, as the great running doctor George Sheehan once said, the difference between a runner and a jogger is not speed, it's a race entry-blank.]

That winter of 1982–83, a running club was organized in Port Jefferson. On the Sunday morning "long run" of 6 to 8 miles I fell in with a local architect named Ed Miller. Having started running only the previous September, Ed was talking about doing the Newsday/Long Island Marathon in the *coming spring*. He had a good training program for it, he told me, a book by Ardy Friedberg called *How to Run Your First Marathon*. I should take a look at it, he said. "Marathoning? Are you crazy? Too much time, too much pain, too little gain," I commented. Again I'm not sure why, but two weeks later I was looking at the program.

By the early spring of 1983 I was planning to do not a marathon but a 20-mile road race south across Long Island from Port Jefferson to Patchogue, in June. I'd use a slightly modified version of the very easy, four-to-five–hours-per-week program that Ardy Friedberg had designed for doing one's first marathon. It worked. I finished that race comfortably—at the back of the pack, but comfortably. I was now definitely on my way to long-distance racing, helped by a really good training program. I planned to do my first marathon in Dallas, Texas (the White Rock), the following December.

The key to the training program for me was that it

was set out in minutes, not miles. Thus, among other things, there's neither speed nor distance pressure built into the program. You're focusing on developing endurance, all you need to finish a long race at a reasonable pace. The program worked for me and eventually became the progenitor of the "Essential Triathlete Training Program," the "Triathloning for Ordinary Mortals Training Program" that appeared in my first book on triathlon.

TRIATHLON THOUGHTS

*W*hile I was training for that first long road race, I was becoming more aware of the existence of that then-new racing sport called triathlon. It combined swimming, biking, and running. The previous year I had seen the February 1982 Hawaii Ironman on television. In that famous race, Julie Moss (who was still racing as of the 1995 season), while leading in the women's division, collapsed a quarter mile before the finish line. While she undertook to crawl toward and eventually across it, she was passed for first place by Kathleen McCartney. To this day anyone, triathlete or no, who saw Julie do what she did still remembers that heroic event. (Ironically, it's unlikely that many remember who Kathleen McCartney was. She disappeared from the sport not long after her win in Hawaii.)

The first triathlon to be held on Long Island had been run the previous September. Then called the "Mighty Hamptons" (and now called "Southampton Hospital Triathlon"), it had been held in Southampton, New York, with the swim in the open Atlantic Ocean. First place on the women's side had been taken by the former New York

City Marathon winner, the then-well-known New Zealand distance runner Allison Roe.

In May 1983, I heard about the second running of the race, this time with the swim course laid out in more protected water near Sag Harbor, New York, to be held in September of that year. I looked at the distances: a 1.5-mile swim, a 25-mile bike, a 10-mile run. "Possibly doable," I said to myself. I estimated how long each leg would take me, and came up with a time, about 4 hours and 20 minutes. It happened to be the same time that I was projecting for my first marathon. Perhaps I could just adapt Ardy's marathon program to doing a triathlon, I thought.

By now I was riding my bike more, as well as running. Although I hadn't swum since childhood, I had been a good (if slow) swimmer back then. But I hadn't liked it much. Nevertheless, my horizons were expanding rapidly. I sent in my application, was accepted, and took to the pool to see if I could still swim.

First time in the pool, I went for 30 minutes. I did 4 laps crawl, 4 laps sidestroke, 4 laps elementary backstroke. Because I was already in decent shape and didn't try to go too fast, I didn't get tired. I soon got my swimming time up to an hour, just a bit less than I figured I'd need to complete the 1.5 miles. I was on my way.

RECOGNIZING LIMITATIONS

*W*hen I had started running back in November 1980, my first goal had been to run a mile without stopping. I achieved that in about a month. Then I set another goal, and achieved it, and another, and achieved it, and another, and so on. Each goal was a reasonable one for both my body and my mind. While I gradually explored my limits, I also recognized my limitations.

I played to my strength, which is endurance, and didn't worry about my weakness, which is lack of foot speed, and bike speed, and swim speed. I've never gone so fast in a race that I've worn myself out. I've never gone so fast in a swim that I got to breathing hard. Even when I've had to drop out of a race, and I've done that a few times, it's never been because I was worn out physically. Rather, it's been because I was too slow and ran out of time, or the weather was dangerously hot, or I was worn out mentally.

If you take up this sport, and approach it in the gradual way I recommend, it's likely that you too will find some strengths and abilities that you never dreamed you had. Many other people have done so. And who knows what level you might reach. I was really surprised when, two years to the day after I finished my first triathlon, I finished my first ironman-distance triathlon, and stopped for lunch while doing it, too.

IRONMAN THOUGHTS

*I*n my case, one race had led to another. I finished my first ironman-distance triathlon, the Cape Cod Endurance, in 16 hours and 42 minutes. My goal had been simply to finish the race within the official time limit of 17 hours. And I did. It didn't matter to me that the winner that day, Scott Tinley, in setting the then–world's record for the distance did it in precisely one-half the time I did. It didn't matter to me that I was the last finisher in regulation time.

What mattered was that I had set a reasonable goal and I had achieved it. I had recognized my limitations in speed, but explored my limits for endurance and found that they were pretty broad.

For me, the ironman distance is *not* the coin of the realm for triathlon. It's simply the most challenging variety of triathlon I've been prepared to take on. Some *non*triathletes may ask you, "Have you ever done a *real* triathlon, you know, Hawaii?" That question reveals only the ignorance of the questioner.

All triathlons are "real" for the triathletes doing them, whatever the distance. The only differences between triathlons are how long they are, and how hilly, windy, or hot they are—not how "real" they are. All triathlons are challenging. Some are just more challenging than others.

If you become a triathlete and never do an ironman, that's only because it's not for you, or you don't have the time, or don't want to spend the time, or don't fancy hurting over some long period of time one fine day. It's not because you're not a real triathlete. Is anyone who hasn't done a *double* ironman not a *real* triathlete?

MAKING MAJOR CHANGE GRADUALLY

*B*y the fall of 1995 I had done more than fifty triathlons, including three at the ironman distance, six other long ones, over twenty at the Standard distance, and close to eighteen Sprints; over twenty duathlons (bike/run events) at various distances; and six marathons, ten half-marathons, a variety of shorter-distance road races, and one 5k swim for good measure. For a for-

mer nonathlete, I had to say to myself, "Good going."
Along the way, I lost about twenty pounds of body fat,
and put on about fifteen pounds of muscle. I lost about
three inches on my waist.

What was my progression? I went from nonexerciser
to 20-minutes-three-times-per-week runner. It took me a
month to get there. Then I moved on to 30 to 40 minutes,
four to five times per week. It was a year and a half before I did my first race, of 5 miles. It was another five
months before I went 10 kilometers (6.2 miles). I spent
about seven months preparing for my first triathlon, and
then another three after that before I did my first
marathon. From then on it was just one race at a time.

In this book, I talk repeatedly about the importance
of making change gradually. Your rate of change may be
slower than mine, or faster. But it is gradual change you
should focus on. Gradual change leads to permanent
changes.

WHERE MIGHT YOU GET TO?

*A*t about that time I had made that first Cobo
Hall–inspired decision to get in shape, I was called to the
Texas College of Osteopathic Medicine as a consultant
by a former radiologist and professor of Medical History
named Charles Ogilvie, D.O. But Charlie did more than
open new vistas for me in medical education: He became
one of my primary inspirations to continue running.

Charlie Ogilvie himself had been sedentary and
about eighty pounds overweight when he took up running at the age of fifty-nine. He went on to become a
truly astonishing athlete. His personal best for the mara-

thon is 3 hours and 3 minutes. That's twenty-six consecutive 7-minute miles. He celebrated his sixty-fifth year by running ten marathons. He almost always won his age class, and was often faster than the winners of the four to five–next younger age groups. At one time he was the North American record holder in his age group for the 10k.

For a change of pace, at sixty-eight Charlie took up triathlon. At sixty-nine, Charlie made *Triathlon Today*'s All-American Triathlon Team for his age group. At that time, Charlie's mother was still living, hale and hearty in her nineties. Her comment when Charlie turned to triathlon was, "Charles. Do you really think it's safe for a man of your age to be riding a bicycle on the public roads?"

Granted, few of us will find within ourselves abilities of this sort at that age (and if we do, we may very well be blessed with a mother of the type Charlie had, too). But you never know. I can tell you from my experience that finding capabilities within yourself that were previously unknown, at whatever level, is enormously rewarding, and may well be for you, as it has been for me, one of the grandest events of your life.

1

WHAT IS A
TRIATHLON?

A triathlon is a race in which three different distance sports are done consecutively. A competitor's finishing time is the cumulative clockings for the three race segments plus the time required to change clothing and equipment between each of the segments. Most commonly, the three sports included are swimming, cycling, and running, and most commonly they're done in that order.

Many people outside the sport think that triathlon is nothing more nor less than the "ironman" seen on television, in which competitors do a 2.4-mile swim, a 112-mile bike, and a 26.2-mile marathon run*. Because this is virtually the only exposure most people get to triathlon, they believe the sport is something they could never participate in. But, while there are a few triathlons that cover those distances, most are much shorter, and much easier to do. And while most triathletes find most of their races demanding, "fun" rather than "grueling" is the word triathletes much more commonly use to describe the experience.

In the mid-'90s, the coin of the realm for triathlon races is, in this book, termed the "Standard" distance (see the preface, pages 12–13). It consists of a 1.5k (0.93-mile) swim, a 40k (24.8-mile) bike, and a 10k (6.2-mile) run. Increasing in popularity and availability are the "Sprints." Not standardized like the Standard-distance races, the variable Sprint race-lengths are generally in the range of a ¼-to-½–mile swim, a 10-to-15–mile bike, and a 3-to-5–mile run. There are also a few races at the "half-ironman" distance, a 1.2-mile swim, a 56-mile bike, and a 13.1-mile run, as well as an occasional one at a length between that and the Standard.

There were few Sprints around when I started out. But as the sport has matured and many race organizers and directors have made a conscious effort to make the sport more accessible and attractive, there are more and more of them on the race calendar. Helping that effort has been the growth of duathlon (formerly called "biathlon"**).

---

*The word "ironman" generically refers to any race at those distances. The term "Ironman," with a capital I, refers to the Ironman Triathlon World Championship in Hawaii (the descendant of the very first race of its kind, held on the island of Oahu in 1978.) Under various sponsorships, the Ironman has been held on the Kona Coast of the Big Island of Hawaii since 1981.

**The term "duathlon" was substituted for the older one, "biathlon," as the international campaign to gain inclusion for the sport in the Olympics got underway. The term "biathlon" is already used in the Olympics to denote a winter Nordic event that combines cross-country skiing and target shooting.

Duathlons are races consisting of running and cycling legs only. But they usually have three segments: a run, a bike, and another run. This gives them something of the "feel" of a triathlon without requiring swimming. Common distances are about 3 miles for each of the run segments, and 15 to 20 miles for the bike. Duathlons are great fun, less time consuming than most triathlons, and a terrific way to get into multisport racing. Easier for most people to contemplate and to do than triathlon, duathlon is now well established, with many races to choose from.

WHAT'S IN IT FOR YOU?

*T*riathletes compete for many reasons. In these colorful, busy, variety-filled races you meet a lot of nice, happy, healthy, friendly people. Most triathletes are just ordinary folks who happen to be exploring their limits, who feel that happiness is not simply accepting life as it is, even if it is indeed good. They know that happiness is also engaging in a process of continuous exploration, discovery, and growth. Triathlon is very much a part of that.

And of course, triathlon training is a great way to get and stay fit and healthy.

A few triathletes have the potential to win a medal, either overall or in their age group. If you have the potential, that's great. Go for it. Being first is a great experience. But most of us don't have that potential. Most of us do triathlons because the training and the racing make us feel good and feel good about ourselves. Crossing the finish line, regardless of when, is simply a thrill in and of itself, every time it happens.

But perhaps the most important reason to triathlon is that after the race you'll likely answer the question "How was it?" the way most triathletes do, whether they've done one race or one hundred: "It was fun!"

No one is sure exactly why triathlons are so much fun for most entrants. After all, "fun" is a word heard infrequently around the finish area of most running road-races of equivalent length. For triathlon, the "fun" aspect is probably related to having to run only a third of the time you're on the course, since you're seated during the bike portion, and during the swim most of your body weight is supported while you exercise. The "fun" is probably also related to the inherent variety of triathlon, to the enforced rest stops of the transitions, and the distractions of many things going on at the same time. These components assure that triathlon racing is never *boring*.

Triathlon is being there and getting there, doing what *you* can do, that first time out training your body and your mind to do something that you've never done before, possibly something you've never before even contemplated doing. That's what counts, and that, too, is what makes triathloning fun.

TRIATHLON AND NOT WINNING

*B*ut, you may be thinking, how can I enter a race knowing I'm not going to win and still have fun? As you know from the prologue, I'm a back-of-the-pack triathlete. In my earlier years, if I came in ahead of a quarter of the other finishers, I felt that I had had an outstanding race. As I get older, I get even slower. Now I'm generally among the last 5 percent of the finishers. The overall winner usually does the race in less than 60 percent of the time that it takes me. I am ordinarily not close even to the winner of my age group. And I still love it every bit as much as I used to.

Perhaps one reason is that triathlon is not like sailboat racing. I did that sport years ago, with very little in the way of trophies to show for my efforts. But in sailboat racing you get no credit for simply going around the course. In triathlon, completing the race is an achievement in itself. In triathlon you always have yourself to compete with, too, if you want competition. And if on a given day you don't, you can just go out, enjoy the weather, the scenery, and the sensations of swimming, biking, and running, at your own comfortable pace.

As with any race, while you do need to be a good athlete to go fast in a triathlon, with very ordinary athletic skills you can compete in triathlons and enjoy the experience for its own sake. For most triathletes, including the winners, the most important skills are the mental ones: the abilities to focus, concentrate, and be disciplined in both the training and the races. Virtually anyone who wants to can develop these skills (see chapters 2 and 3).

SPEED AND DOING A TRIATHLON

Speed is determined only in part by the amount and type of training you do. A lot of it has to do with natural ability. If you're naturally faster than someone else, and spend the same amount of time training that he does, you'll cover more miles in your training. And it's likely that you're going to go faster in the races. If you're interested, you can also learn to go faster by doing what's called "speed training." But speed is not at all essential for finishing a triathlon.

As I stated in the preface, if you can swim a mile in 45 minutes, bike 25 miles in 2 hours, and run a 10k in 65 minutes (these are fairly slow times—around my pace), and if you don't take too long in transition, you can do a Standard-distance triathlon in around 4 hours and the average Sprint in 2 hours or less. And if you make those times, the chances are very good that you won't be last.

By the way, while you might think that being last is no fun at all, actually, being last is great fun. Everyone makes a fuss over you. You're something of a celebrity. You're noticed: "You did it! You hung in there! Good going!" It's being *next* to last that's not so much fun. Then you're completely anonymous.

IS FINISHING EVERYTHING, THEN?

*N*o, not even finishing is everything. As Dave Scott, who won the Hawaii Ironman six times in the 1980s and then at age forty came out of a several-years' retirement from competitive racing to finish second in 1994, said (in 1985): "I encourage all . . . triathletes to reach for your goals, whether they be to win or just to try. The trying is everything."

Just being there and doing the best you can do on that particular day makes you feel good, even if you don't finish. Suppose it's very hot, or it's raining, or there are a lot of hills on the bike or the run, or the swim is in rough water. Or suppose you're just plain tired, or your head's not in it and you can't concentrate on the race. There are many reasons why a person might not finish on a particular day.

Not finishing is an experience that many of us have had. But if you focus on the fact that you trained and got out there, if you focus on what you *did* do that day, not what you *didn't* do, it still will be a good experience for you. And remember, there's always another race.

EXPERIENCE AND DOING YOUR FIRST TRIATHLON

*D*oing a triathlon takes more than training and conditioning. It also takes some planning and logistics management. It helps to have some racing experience in one or more of the triathlon sports. Maybe you've done a few 5k or 10k running road-races, or competed in a local Masters swim meet or two, or have tried a bike time-trial or even a criterium event.

Having been through the experience of entering, getting to the race, parking conveniently, registering, making sure that all your equipment is there and in order, lining up for a mass swim start, and so on—in a race that has fewer details to remember than a triathlon does—is a plus. It will certainly help you to deal with some of the butterflies that you'll naturally feel before the start of your first triathlon. *Such experience is not essential, however.* For many triathletes, their first triathlon has been their first race of any kind.

WHAT ABOUT EQUIPMENT?

You may be thinking, "Won't I need a lot of equipment, especially one of those expensive bikes with a set of those funny-looking handlebars and a disk wheel?" Well, no. It may look like you have a lot to buy, but you really don't. Only a few of the items—bike, bike helmet, and running shoes—are must purchases if you don't already own them. Once you get going, you can gradually expand your inventory of first-line triathlon equipment.

As for the bike, you definitely *don't* need to start off with one of those expensive ones designed specifically to facilitate going fast in a triathlon, and in fact shouldn't. If you just want to try your luck the first time out without making any major investments, virtually any bike with a gearshift mechanism will do. If you have access to a road bike (a modern version of the old "ten-speed"), or a common garden-variety mountain bike, or a "combi" or "hybrid" (a road bike with upright handlebars and slightly wider tires), you can do just fine on it.

Plenty of people begin that way. And some use just about anything with two wheels, handlebars, a chain, and pedals mounted on a bike frame. Bill Crosby did the very first race I was in, the 1983 Mighty Hamptons, using a lady's Raleigh with a full chain case, a three-speed Sturmey-Archer shifter, and a wicker basket on the handlebars. First-time duathlete Nita Zackson did the first race I was in for the 1995 season, the Queens Biathlon, on a mountain bike with a luggage rack and saddlebags attached.

Alternatively, you can go out and buy a decent entry-level road bike. (Details and guidelines for purchasing a new bike are outlined in chapter 6.)

As for additional equipment, on the bike you'll be required to wear an approved bike helmet. Every bike helmet has a little sticker on the headliner certifying the fact that it meets the standards of one or more of the approving agencies. When you buy your helmet, just make sure that it has at least one of the requisite stickers. By the way, pick another race if you find one that doesn't require a helmet; it can't be protected by liability insurance.

You can use your running shoes on the bike, but as you become a more experienced cyclist you'll probably want to get bike shoes, cleats, and racing pedals. Combined, these pieces of equipment increase your mechanical advantage significantly. (Further details on accessories are outlined in chapter 6.)

For the swim, you'll obviously need a swimsuit. Most triathletes either keep their suit on for the bike and the run, putting biking and/or running shorts on over them, or, since Lycra dries very quickly, wear their bike/run outfit during the swim. You'll also need a pair of swim goggles, and you may want to use earplugs. Virtually all of the races require a swim cap. Most supply you with it, but some require you to bring or buy one. Many triathletes wear a wetsuit. It protects you against the cold in cold-water swims, and, by increasing buoyancy and reducing friction, increases your speed under any conditions. However, this item is expensive and not essential as long as the water temperature is above approximately 68° F. Once you become a committed triathlete, you can consider adding a wetsuit to your wardrobe.

For the run, you'll need a good, well-fitting pair of running shoes, shorts (if you don't wear your swimsuit or bike shorts), and a T-shirt or singlet (tank top). (For more details on equipment matters, see chapter 6.)

DEALING WITH SOME OBSTACLES TO BECOMING A MULTISPORT RACER

In Swimming

Suppose you know how to swim, and you want to start off your multisport racing experience with a triathlon, but you're not sure that you could do the racing crawl for the whole distance. No problem. Any stroke is legal in the swim segment. You can use backstroke, sidestroke, breaststroke, or anything else you can think of. And you can use them in combination. Let's say that you can swim the crawl for ¼ mile at a time. You could then take a breather doing an easy sidestroke and get back to the crawl when you're comfortable.

If you don't know how, but would like to try it, there are many places where you can learn how to swim or learn how to swim better. The local "Y," a health club with a swimming pool, and universities or schools that have pools often have learn-to-swim programs. You could also consider getting private instruction from a swim coach or trainer. You can find such people through a local swim program or sporting-goods store that services triathletes. If you really don't like to swim or don't want to or can't take the time to learn, there is, of course, duathlon. (For more on swimming and other triathlon sports techniques, see chapter 5.)

In Running

If you don't like to or can't run, you will be pleased to know that walking is perfectly legal in the run segment of both duathlons and triathlons. You can just do an ordinary walk, as fast as you can. Or, if you know how, you can use the formal racewalking gait. But while it can be fast (how does a 7-minute mile sound?), that technique takes some time to learn and has strict rules.

There is an easy fast-walking gait that falls between ordinary walking and racewalking. The gait is "Pace-Walking," also known as striding, speed walking, power walking, aerobic walking, and fitness walking, among other terms. I have done it in a number of triathlons, and in the 1989 New York City Marathon, using it I managed sub–11-minute miles for the distance, not too far off my personal-best running.

At a brisk pace, with ordinary walking you can cover a mile in about 15 minutes. But if you use one of the athletic walking gaits, you can increase your speed considerably, while still experiencing much less wear and tear than you do when running. There's no secret here. In any walking gait, by definition your rear foot is still on the ground when your front foot comes down. In running, with each step there's always an instant when you're airborne. Thus, in walking the weight-bearing is split with each step, sharply diminishing the jarring and pounding that for many people accompanies running. (For details on running and PaceWalking techniques, see chapter 5.)

HOW MUCH YOU NEED TO TRAIN

*Y*ou may have heard that to do one of these events, even a short one, you have to train a lot. You may have heard the figure fifteen to twenty hours per week, for most of the year. Some triathletes follow that sort of schedule. But how much you need to train depends entirely on *what* you're training *for*.

If you're just out to have fun triathloning, you don't have to train nearly that much. Assuming that you're not out to win your age group, you can very comfortably do your first Standard-distance race, and certainly your first Sprint, on a program in which you average only five hours of training per week for only thirteen weeks before the race—total, for all three sports. That's assuming you've established a reasonable "aerobic base" for at least three months before you start. (You'll find the Essential Triathlete Training Program (ETTP) outlined in chapter 3.)

Many triathletes who have used the training program outlined in this book, or other similar training programs that prescribe the five-to-six–hours-a-week workout schedule, have been able to compete and finish their triathlons to their satisfaction year after year. Recreational marathoners have been using an equivalent training program for years. Such a program is designed not to enable you to win in your age division—though, of course, you may—but to enable you to compete and finish and have fun doing it. If you like what you're doing and are happy with your performance, there's no need to increase the amount of time you devote to training.

Some people think that the "real" triathletes are only those who go fast and train for at least fifteen hours per week. For example, Sally Edwards, to her credit one of the pioneer triathletes and early popularizers of the sport, once (in 1988) defined what she called a "triathloid": a "bozo who prefers to survive, rather than train for, triathlons."

Sally's own recommended training program from that period *began* at six hours per week (close to where the ETTP maxes out) and built up to *twenty-two to twenty-five* hours per week (1982). Such a training program can produce triathletes who can go both fast and long, but very few people have that amount of time to devote to training, much less the inclination to do so. Advocating such a program thus becomes exclusionary.

A triathlete and triathlon journalist, Mike Plant, presented a training program for the "Beginning Triathlete" (1988) that required a minimum of eleven to twelve hours per week (for an unspecified number of weeks). His program for the "Advanced Triathlete" required a minimum of seventeen and a half hours per week. Mike then allowed that "neither of the training programs shown here is going to get you through the Ironman."

Well, the training programs that Mike Plant offered might not have gotten *him* through the ironman at the speeds he would have been satisfied with, but I can tell you from my own experience that an ironman can be done, at a reasonable, comfortable pace, on less training than is required by even his "Beginning Triathlete" program (see chapter 8).

I take issue with the positions of triathlete-writers like Sally Edwards and Mike Plant because I think a "good" triathlete isn't necessarily a "fast" one. I believe, both as a professional in preventive medicine and as a triathlete, that this great, healthy, fun sport should be made available and attractive to everyone who wishes to participate.

Training for triathlon is a very healthy way to do aerobic exercise, which has so many physical and mental benefits. Telling folks that they have to train a minimum of ten to fifteen hours per week just to get out on the course puts them off, unnecessarily.

The average recreational runner in this country does 12 to 15 miles per week, working out for about two to three hours per week. The average middle-of-the-pack 10k racer probably does 20 to 25 miles per week, although no one knows for sure. That's three to four hours per week. If you want to do a triathlon fast, you do have to train a good deal more than that and throw in some speed training. But to just get out there and have a good time, adding an hour or two per week will do the trick.

Don't get me wrong. I think that fast and winning are great. If you can go fast and win, without getting injured, and without making a shambles of the rest of your life while you're training, great. Go for it. But in triathlon "good" ought to be defined by what each individual reasonably *wants* to do and *can* do—while maintaining and improving his physical and mental health.

I've spent much triathlon time in the back of the pack, and believe me, I've never seen any "bozos" or "triathloids" back there. Only triathletes and duathletes, doing their best.

In the spring of 1988 I heard a talk by Dr. George Sheehan, the late, great philosopher-physician of running. He described his experience, as he got older and as he recovered from a serious illness, of doing 10k races at an 8-to-9–minutes-per-mile pace rather than his customary 6-to-7–minutes-per-mile pace. Over the years, George had inspired masses of runners, because of his talent, determination, and wisdom. In his own races he had often won or placed in his age class. Thus he had spent little time among the "ordinary" runners. But in that talk, that day, he told us that coming to run back there had let him see who the "real heroes" of road racing are.

I've heard top triathletes express amazement at the ability of back-of-the-packers to stay out on the course for as long as we do, especially on a hot day. These are correct attitudes. Both fast and long in triathlon require special, if different, abilities. Both the fast and the long are "real" triathletes.

A Special Category in Triathlon

The "Clydesdale Division"

Some years ago I received a call from Maryland's Joseph Law, who had a very good idea. Joe, who weighed about 200 pounds, had been encouraging race directors to set up weight as well as age divisions for awards. Joe had collected a great deal of data on race performance by weight. He concluded that once out of the water, heavier triathletes are at a disadvantage compared with their lighter colleagues when it comes to winning or placing in the age groups. His idea was to encourage heavier folks to try the endurance sports by offering them special opportunities to earn an award in triathlon.

As so, on May 29, 1988, for the Columbia, Maryland, triathlon, Joe was able to arrange for men's and women's heavyweight divisions. The lower limits were 195 pounds for men, 145 pounds for women. Within the heavyweight division there were two age classes: under forty, and forty and above. The experiment was a success and fun for all. From that start has come the "Clydesdale Division" that's now part of a number of races.

References

Edwards, S. *Triathlon*. Sacramento, CA: Fleet Feet Press, 1982.

Edwards, S. "From the Editors." In *Triathlete*, July 1988, p. 2.

Plant, M. "The *Perfect* Cross-Training Week." In *Runner's World*, May 1988, p. 51.

Scott, D. "Finish Line." In *Triathlon*, December/January 1985, p. 80.

2

THE MENTAL ASPECTS OF TRIATHLON

*T*he renowned American inventor Thomas Alva Edison said: "Invention is 10 percent inspiration, 90 percent perspiration." Taking the word "inspiration" to signify mental work, at first blush one might think that the same ratio would apply to triathlon: not too much brain, a lot of brawn. It happens that this isn't the case. In triathlon racing, even on a very hot day the ratio between mental and physical work is rather different from the one Edison set forth for the process of invention.

Some time back, Mark Allen, who won the Hawaii Ironman five consecutive times through 1993, described winning that race as a "mental exercise in pain management." For recreational triathletes doing Sprint or Standard-distance races, "pain management" only occasionally becomes an issue. But in any triathlon, mental work is at least as important as physical work. The longer the race is, the more important your mind power becomes in relation to your body power. And certainly the key element in making sure that you're adequately *trained* to do the race you've chosen is mental discipline.

YOUR MIND IN TRAINING

*T*he power and importance of the mind in triathlon is nowhere more evident than in training. You need to be able to go out for a scheduled workout in the morning when you awaken feeling groggy, as well as when you awaken full of vim and vigor. You need to be able to go to the pool at the end of a particularly hard day's work to put in the yards or the minutes you need on the swim. Even at five to six hours of training per week, there are still times when you've got to get out there when you really don't want to. That requires discipline.

The power of the mind is also evident in the discipline you need in order not to *over*train. Knowing when enough is enough, to achieve the results you want. Being aware that overdoing it can, at times, be more harmful than underdoing it in terms of potential long-term damage to your body and thus your racing career. And even when your training as well as your racing season are going well, you need the mental discipline to say to yourself, as you should from time to time, "Let's take it easy this week," or even, "Let's take the week off." Physical conditioning won't disappear overnight and sometimes the best thing you can do for your muscles and your mind is to give them both some rest.

IN THE RACES

Logistics

You also need to use your mind in planning for your races, something we'll get into in detail in chapter 7. Triathlons and, to a lesser extent, duathlons require a good degree of logistical organization, certainly much more than a single-sport race does. After thirteen seasons of triathlon racing, each time I pack up for a race I still refer to my checklist of clothing and equipment. If I don't, I'm almost sure to forget to bring something important.

Focus and Concentration

Mental discipline is important in the races as well, of course. Central to finishing, especially in the long races (whatever a long race is for *you*, whether at the Sprint, Standard-distance, half-iron, or ironman distance), is the ability to focus, to concentrate. It's the ability to keep your eye on the prize: for most of us, finishing in our desired time.

Focus and concentration also means keeping your wits about you during the race (and while you're out training as well). It means staying alert, and out of harm's way from traffic, natural hazards, and other racers. Even when you're tired, you need to be able to think clearly, to remember to drink and eat at the required frequencies. In hot weather, drinking fluids on a regular basis *before* you get thirsty is vital. You have to *remember* to do it. Slowing down at a water stop when you're going well, feeling good, and not experiencing thirst requires mental discipline. If during a race or workout, you wait to drink until you get thirsty, you've waited too long and you won't be able to catch up with your body's need for fluids.

Not Going TOO Fast

For most of us, learning not to go too fast in a race is more important than training up so that we won't be going slower than we want to. If you go too fast at the beginning, you can wear yourself out, be unable to finish, and/or get injured. It's tempting to go fast right at the start of each race segment, when the adrenaline is flowing. It's also easy to get carried away and power yourself all the way through the bike leg because you're a good cyclist, you're feeling good that day, and you get caught up in some person-on-person competition at a given level. Many times after a race I've heard someone say: "If only I had held back a bit on the bike. I just had nothing left for the run." Discipline is what you need for controlling that urge. From your training you must learn just how fast you can comfortably go in each event, and then shoot for that. Don't overshoot.

For example, when I'm swimming, my heart rate is rarely up in my aerobic range. (For a definition of "aerobic range," see pages 69–70.) I do a mile in about 40 minutes without a wetsuit in calm, fresh water. (I go a bit faster in salt water with a wetsuit on.) That's fairly slow, but I accept the speed and enjoy the swim, because I don't enjoy feeling even a bit short of breath in the water. I may be slow, but I never feel uncomfortable. I've the same approach to the bike and the run or PaceWalk. If you stay at race paces that are comfortable and doable, you vastly increase your chances of success.

You may even want to plan rest stops during the race—in the transitions, or out on the bike and run courses. (I did that in my first ironman-distance race back in 1985. I took 20-minute transitions. I stopped for lunch at a fast-food restaurant. I got off the bike for 2 minutes at every 10-mile aid station. I probably added about an hour to my total time. But I made my objective, which was to beat the 17-hour time limit. And I might not have been able to do that without the rest stops.)

Knowing When to Stop

Finally, in the races the power of the mind comes in knowing when to stop, when to take a Did Not Finish, if you have to. You must be able to recognize when it's just too hot, or when the headwind is too strong, or that you really didn't take enough long rides to prepare properly for the race, or that you don't have enough time left in the race to make the time limit, or that you just don't have it in general that day. (I've experienced all of the above.)

You must be able to recall why you're doing multisport racing (and assuming you're not a pro, if it's primarily for some reason other than having fun, I would rethink the whole deal). You must be able to stop *before* you get heatstroke, or hypothermia, or a serious musculoskeletal injury. Remember, in the scorecard of life, no one was ever declared a failure for not finishing a particular race on a particular day. And remember too, there's always another race.

MOTIVATION

*N*ow, if you're going to get to the stage where you're effectively using your mind in training and in racing, you must first be motivated to start training to do that first race, and then perhaps go on to become a regular triathlete. In other words, you must first get motivated.

Technically, motivation is the state of mind characterized as an emotion, feeling, desire, idea, or intellectual understanding; or a psychological, physiological, or health need mediated by a mental process that leads to the taking of one or more actions. Motivation is essential to self-preservation and the underlying human striving to be healthy.

If you're reading this book, you're probably already motivated to try triathlon racing. But if that's not the case, and you're simply exploring the possibility for now, you might be facing one or more of these common roadblocks: "I really don't want to do this," "I know I'll just never be able to get started," "I just know I don't have the time," "One day I'll want to and the next day I won't," or fear of failure once you do get started.

In most cases there's a reason *why* someone "gets motivated" to do something. But "getting motivated" is not a question of finding the magic *outside* of yourself and somehow bringing it inside. Getting motivated is rather a matter of finding a presently quiescent force *inside* yourself. In most cases, the type of reasoning that comes from within, such as, "I want to do this for me, to challenge myself, to help me to feel better physically, and to feel better about myself," is a much more effective motivator than the external type of reasoning, such as, "I'm doing this for my (spouse, boy/girlfriend, children/parents, employer/coworkers)." Invariably, being motivated to embark on something like triathlon racing in order to impress or please someone besides yourself leads to guilt, anxiety, anger, frustration, and then, often, to injury and/or quitting. In the long run it will be best to do this for *you*. In any case, guilt is a lousy long-term motivator.

Taking Control

When you take control, you have decided what you want to do with your body, perhaps to do something you've never done or never even contemplated doing before. Then you go out and do it.

There are many choices for the previously physically inactive person to make, opportunities to take control, just in starting down the pathway of regular exercise, much less in undertaking to do a triathlon. For the regular exerciser/single-sport racer contemplating multisport racing, these are similar choices to make.

Whether to undertake a change process at all. *What* goals to set. *Which* sport(s) and activity(s) to engage in. Making choices, of course, means taking responsibility for yourself. Taking control and taking responsibility are both mental processes known to psychologists to be very powerful motivational tools. And, having a menu of choices is itself known to be an important element in mobilizing motivation.

Ambivalence

Even the most highly motivated, disciplined, and focused triathlete may feel like not training on a particular day, like not finishing a particular race, even like dropping out of the sport completely. This feeling of ambivalence, the "state of mind characterized by coexisting but conflicting feelings about a contemplated action, another person, or a situation in which one finds oneself" (Miller and Rollnick, 1991, p. 38), is perfectly normal. Virtually everyone who even thinks about making a major change in his life experiences it. As does virtually every triathlete more than once during his career in the sport. I certainly have.

The key to success in dealing with ambivalence is to accept that it will always be present to some extent. Sometimes the ambivalent feelings will be weaker, sometimes stronger. What you *do* in response to the feelings determines their impact, determines whether they'll trip you up or not get in your way. If ambivalence destroys your commitment, that's one thing, but if it simply questions your commitment, if it does nothing more than take you on a temporary detour, it can lead to a strengthening of resolve to proceed forward.

Fighting or ignoring feelings of ambivalence doesn't work in most cases. Rather, go with the flow. If you really feel like taking that training day off, or dropping out of that race, that season, forever even, try to understand why you feel this way. If you're tired, take a break—your body may be telling you it needs some time off. If after your break you don't want to resume for now, don't fight it. You are, or should be, in this to have fun. When it stops being fun, it's time to stop doing it.

ANALYZING AND MANAGING PAIN

You'll need to learn to know your body. For example, you'll learn from experience when the pain you're feeling at a given time in a training session or a race is from muscle use, and not from an injury. Then you'll know that when you finish your workout or your race, or perhaps even when you go on to the next race segment, it will go away. Pain management is being able to act on that knowledge and keep going. You might push through the pain without slowing down or you might say to yourself, "It's okay, I can handle going a minute-a-mile slower on the run in terms of where I finish; it's going to hurt a *lot* less and that's worth it."

Several times in long races, on the bike segment, I've experienced a good deal of knee pain. I was able to deal with it because I was pretty sure that it was just from exertion. I was almost certain that it would go away on the run, when I'd be using different muscles. And indeed it did. If it had been there when I went out on my next ride (it wasn't), I surely would have had it looked at. Learning pain management comes from experience. Over time you'll learn about your body, what it can handle, and when you need to back off. (For more information on injury, see page 125.)

GOAL SETTING

*F*inally, we come to perhaps the most important kind of mind-work you have to do in order to be a successful triathlete in your own terms: goal setting. What is it that you want to do in triathlon and why do you want to do it? What is it that you're reasonably capable of doing, given your athletic history and your reasonably achievable level of physical conditioning? Before you swim a stroke, push a pedal, take a step, to become a triathlete you need to have it very clear in your head just what you want to accomplish and why you want to accomplish it.

Do you want to finish, to go fast, to place in your age

group, to win the race overall? Is finishing in the middle to the back-of-the-pack acceptable? Is last okay, just as long as you finish? Depending upon your commitment, your available time, and your natural ability, any of these may be a reasonable goal.

Realism

To set goals that are going to work for you, the goals you set must be realistic ones—for you. There's a strong genetic component in the determination of body shape and size, such as one's innate speed potential or one's innate potential for significantly increasing muscle bulk by lifting weights. The goals you set for yourself should be suitable. In the weight-loss context, for example, this does not necessarily mean "getting thin" in the society/media definition. It can very well simply mean getting "thin*ner*."

As I noted earlier, if you're not inherently fast, don't worry yourself about placing in your age group. Not, that is, unless you're prepared to spend a lot of time in speed training (and even that may not do the trick), or are old enough so that in a given race there are three or fewer people in your class and all you have to do to get an award is finish! Remember, going fast is the product of training *plus* natural ability. Many people simply will not be able to go very fast no matter how hard they try. To avoid frustration, injury, and the urge to quit, that fact should be recognized.

In sum, whatever your goals are, identifying them, understanding why you want to achieve them, and making sure that they are reasonable ones for you are absolutely central to achieving success in triathlon. Now let's move on to taking those first steps in achieving the goals you've set for yourself: starting your training program.

REFERENCES

Curry, S. J., and E. H. Wagner. "Evaluation of intrinsic and extrinsic motivation interventions with a self-help smoking cessation program." In the *Journal of Consulting and Clinical Psychology* 59, 1991, p. 318.

Miller, W. R., and S. Rollnick. *Motivational Interviewing: Preparing People to Change Addictive Behavior.* New York: The Guilford Press, 1991.

3

TRAINING
PRINCIPLES
AND PROGRAM

THE PRINCIPLES
OF TRAINING

*A*s a first-timer, you're motivated, you're ready to go, you're all fired up. You're going to do your first multisport event, either a triathlon or a duathlon. Or, as someone who has already done a race or two or more, you're looking to develop a more organized, more time-efficient, more productive approach to the sport.

As either a beginner or a sometime recreational triathlete, you know that you have to train. We've talked a bit about training in general terms, in the preface and chapter 1. You thus know that you have to work out consistently and regularly for some minimum number of weeks. You also know that in order to simply finish a Sprint or Standard-distance triathlon or a duathlon of equivalent distance, the total time you need to spend won't be inordinate. You won't have to turn your life upside down in order to achieve that goal.

Now it's time for some specifics. Three of the four Essential Triathlete Training Program (ETTP) workout schedules are presented in this chapter: the Foundation, the Standard-distance, and the Maintenance. Each is thirteen weeks in length. (The Ironman-distance Triathlon Training Program is provided in chapter 8.)

Following the Standard-distance Triathlon Training Program (Table 3-2) will prepare you for that first race, assuming that you're already reasonably fit and working out regularly for two and a half to three hours per week. If you're not yet at that level, even if you're starting from scratch, in thirteen weeks the Foundation Triathlon Training Program (Table 3-1) will have enabled you to work up to it. This means that if you're starting from scratch and begin your training in March, you can be racing by Labor Day. The Maintenance Triathlon Training Program (Table 3-4) will help you to stay in shape during the off-season. If you're already a multisport racer, but want to find that more focused, balanced approach to training, the Standard-distance Program should work well for you, too.

The Bowerman Principles

Each element of the ETTP is based on precepts set down some years ago by the world-renowned running coach from Oregon, Bill Bowerman (Walsh, 1983). Coach Bowerman, who trained many of the top U.S. middle-distance runners of his time, established Ten Principles for race preparation. Seven of the eight Principles of the ETTP are adapted from his Ten (the last is my contribution to it):

1. Training must be regular, according to a long-term plan.

2. The watchword is moderation.

3. The workload must be balanced, and overtraining must be avoided.

4. Goals should be clearly established. They must be understood, and they must be realistic.

5. Training schedules should be set up with a hard/easy rotation, both from day to day and more generally over time.

6. Regular rest should be scheduled.

7. Whenever possible, working out should be fun.

8. Gradual change leads to permanent changes.

Gradual Change

Number 8 in the list is an aphorism I always like to repeat because it has worked for me over many years. For example, take the Foundation program. The hardier soul may move through this regimen more quickly than I suggest and be ready to start the ETTP after, say, nine weeks rather than thirteen. (Ardy Friedberg's *How to Run Your First Marathon* training program [1982] required only twenty-four weeks from scratch to participation in a full marathon, and was used by thousands of first-timers.) But it's a bad idea to go out for an hour, at full tilt, on that first day, or even on the fifth or the eighth.

For most people too much, too soon is bound to lead to muscle pain, perhaps injury, and an increased likelihood of quitting. *Gradual* increases in time spent, distance covered, and speed comprise the proven formula for sticking with it and developing your body and mind for happy, healthy triathloning. Which brings us to "regularity" and "consistency."

Regularity

The term "regularity" refers to the distribution of training sessions during the week and the distribution of workout weeks over the course of the year. Both should be fairly even. It's a good idea to follow the suggested training-session plan fairly closely.

For example, the Maintenance program provides for an average of three hours per week workout time. You could meet this requirement by working out for an hour on Saturday and 2 hours on Sunday. However, this approach would benefit neither your musculoskeletal nor your cardiovascular conditioning nearly as much as a more regular distribution of shorter workouts would. Furthermore, if your heart rate were to reach a really high level on the weekends only, which it might if you trained only then, you could significantly increase your risk of developing a serious heart problem during exercise.

Your muscles could be harmed by such an approach, too. Muscles worked out on a regular basis on alternate days go through a cycle of buildup, breakdown, and further buildup, leading to increased strength and endurance. Intermittent workouts generally don't lead to the achievement of those ends. Pain and stiffness are the more likely outcomes of such an approach.

Consistency

Consistency refers to workout-session length. As indicated by each of the ETTP components, I recommend that you not vary length of time widely from one session to the next (for instance, training for 15 minutes one day, and an hour and a half the next). For reasons similar to those that militate against irregularity in training, inconsistency can interfere with the development of both musculoskeletal and cardiovascular fitness, and significantly increase the risk of both injury and illness.

Rest

Neither consistency nor regularity is contradicted by regularly scheduled rest. Note the days off that are part of each training program, following Bowerman Principle 6. If you're starting from scratch, and have begun early enough in the season to be able to allow for a week off between completing the Foundation program and commencing the Standard-distance program, and can still make your intended first race, that would be a good idea. Certainly, after you've finished your season, even your first one if you've trained consistently and regularly, take a week or two or even three off before beginning your Maintenance program for the off-season. I always do. You'll give both your body and your mind a much-needed rest. And if you're a recreational triathlete already, a week's downtime at midseason has much to recommend it. Despite what you may have read elsewhere, once you're in shape, while you'll lose some, you won't lose a lot of your conditioning. And both your mind and your body will be much the better for it.

MEDICAL CLEARANCE

Ordinarily, a normal, healthy adult does not need any special medical clearance to begin either the Foundation or the Standard-distance training program. Each program begins with a fairly low level of regular exercise in terms of both time and intensity. That means that if you're going to experience any exercise-related health problems you'll discover this early on, before you have a chance to get into real trouble.

However, it's always better to be on the safe side. And so, if you have any thoughts that you might have a disease or condition that would increase your risk of an adverse event if you were to exercise, it's a good idea to be checked out by your physician before you begin training.

If you have a history of any of the following diseases or conditions, you will *definitely* want to have a thorough medical evaluation before starting either one of the programs:

1. Previous myocardial infarction (heart attack).

2. Chest pain, pressure in the chest, or severe shortness of breath upon exertion.

3. Any history of pulmonary (lung) disease, especially what is called chronic obstructive pulmonary disease (COPD).

4. Any bone, joint, or other diseases or limitations affecting your muscles or skeletal system.

If you have a history of any of the following conditions or lifestyle habits, having a thorough medical evaluation before starting either one of the programs is a good idea:

1. High serum cholesterol.

2. Cigarette smoking.

3. Hypertension.

4. Abuse of drugs or alcohol.

5. Prescribed medication used on a regular basis.

6. Overweight or severe underweight.

7. Any other chronic illness, such as diabetes.

Now, if you do have one or more of the health conditions or problems listed above, you shouldn't necessarily be discouraged. It happens that regular exercise is useful in the management of a number of them. (It's also useful in managing certain dysfunctional psychological states such as mild depression, mild anxiety, and lowered self-esteem.)

If, following an evaluation, your regular physician or other health professional says "no," but you really feel the answer should be "yes," or if you've gotten an answer that doesn't quite seem to make sense, seek a second opinion. Not all health professionals know a great deal about regular exercise and its health benefits.

In many cases the key word for healthy exercising is *care:* A person who is not entirely healthy may embark upon a program of regular exercise, with *care*. If you do have one or more of the above-listed diseases or conditions, and if you make the decision to go ahead, with or without consulting a health professional (the latter is *not* recommended), you should plan a slow, gradual, and *careful* beginning. Then if you experience any increase in untoward symptoms characteristic of your underlying disease or condition, you should definitely and promptly seek a medical evaluation.

Cardiac Stress Testing

For years certain exercise authorities have been recommending that virtually all persons embarking on regular exercise programs, especially programs as relatively vigorous as triathlon training, first undergo cardiac stress testing. However, according to the U.S. Preventive Services Task Force of the United States Public Health Service, there's no evidence that for an adult with no symptoms, getting an electrocardiogram (EKG), of either the resting or treadmill variety, is either necessary or useful in reducing the risk of a negative outcome during regular exercise.

The one exception to that rule is the group of males over forty who have two or more risk factors for heart attack, such as elevated serum cholesterol, a history of cigarette smoking, hypertension, diabetes mellitus, overweight, or a family history of early-onset heart disease. If you're in this group, having a cardiac stress test before starting to train for your first multisport event is a good idea.

STARTING FROM SCRATCH

*I*f you've never exercised on a regular basis, or have done so only intermittently, or are a former regular exerciser who has laid off for a year or more, you should start with the Foundation Triathlon Training Program (Table 3-1). It's designed to enable you to reach a level of fitness from which you can then undertake the Standard-distance Triathlon Training Program with every expectation that you'll be able to complete it and finish your first race.

TABLE 3-1

The Foundation Triathlon Training Program

Day:	M	T	W	Th	F	S	S	Total
W E E K			*(T I M E S I N M I N U T E S)*					
1	Off	20	Off	20	Off	Off	20	60
2	Off	20	Off	30	Off	Off	30	80
3	Off	20	Off	20	Off	30	30	100
4	Off	30	Off	30	Off	30	30	120
5	Off	30	Off	30	Off	40	40	140
6	Off	40	Off	40	Off	40	40	160
7	Off	40	Off	40	Off	40	60	180
8	Off	30	40	30	Off	40	60	200
9	Off	30	40	40	Off	50	60	220
10	Off	40	40	40	Off	60	60	240
11	Off	40	50	40	Off	60	70	260
12	Off	40	60	50	Off	60	70	280
13	Off	50	60	60	Off	70	60	300

All of the programs of the ETTP are laid out in minutes, not miles. Their primary objective is to build up your physical and mental endurance, so that you can eventually be out on the course for the 2 to 4 hours that it will take the slower triathlete to finish a Sprint or Standard-distance race. Obviously, the faster your training paces, the more miles you'll cover and the faster you'll be able to go in the race. But it's the time spent, with consistency and regularity, that's the key to success with this training program.

Obviously, to do a triathlon, you need to be able to swim, bike, and run. But you don't have to be able to do all three with complete proficiency in order to get started on the Foundation program. If necessary, you can use some of your training sessions to practice the swim strokes you're learning at the local "Y" or other venue, and to become more proficient on the bike (see chapter 5).

In fact, you're well advised to spend the first four weeks or so of the Foundation program just running or fast walking (if you're planning to use that gait on the run leg of your first race). That way, being a bit shaky in one or both of the more technical sports will not stand in the way of your beginning to develop your fitness, which should be your objective at this point in any case. Also, whatever sport(s) you are doing, ease into your training. Don't try to go too fast. Just spend those first two to four weeks loosening up and getting used to a routine of regular workouts. Later there will be plenty of time to become more rigorous and vigorous.

Notice that this program very gradually increases both the frequency of your workouts (from three to five times weekly), and the time spent in each one (from 20 minutes to a maximum of 70). It generally follows the Bill Bowerman hard/easy principle. By the time you finish the thirteen weeks, you'll be doing five hours per week, the average for the Standard-distance program, and you'll have averaged three hours per week while getting there. As you add in cycling and swimming, perhaps beginning in week five, you can decide for yourself which workout sessions to devote to each sport. I suggest getting into a pattern in which you're doing each sport at least once a week. A common split for a five-workouts-per-week schedule is one swim, two bike, two run. Since the workouts are all denominated in minutes, in terms of your overall conditioning the sports are interchangeable.

Especially if you're just starting out, this is likely to be an exciting time of self-discovery. Remember, gradual change leads to permanent changes; consistency and regularity are essential to success. As long as you don't try to do too much too soon, you're going to enjoy the process, and you'll greatly diminish the likelihood of getting injured. Enjoyment and staying healthy are the keys to getting to the next level. Stick with the program, focus, and you'll get there.

PREPARING TO RACE: THE ESSENTIAL TRIATHLETE TRAINING PROGRAM

*N*ow you're ready to begin the Standard-distance Triathlon Training Program. Remember that I suggest that for your first race as a beginner, and indeed for every race you enter as a beginning recreational multisport athlete, your goal should be simply to finish. As a recreational multisport racer, after you finish that first one—or two, or three—you may want to think about setting some reasonable time goal now and then, just to add some spice.

But any time goal that you set should be achievable through concentration and maintenance of a steady pace, without (figuratively or literally) killing yourself. The pace you wish to maintain determines your training. The idea is to train at a reasonable pace for a reasonable amount of time that is calculated to make sure you're able to keep going on the course and achieve your primary goal. That's what the ETTP is all about.

Once again, in the Standard-distance program it's the minutes, not the miles, that count. I hardly ever know how many miles I cover in training and don't often care. In this program there are six workouts per week, up one from the frequency of the last six weeks of the Foundation program. They're spread over five days: Tuesday, Wednesday, Friday, Saturday, and Sunday. The two-a-days are generally on Tuesdays. That arrangement assumes that you'll do a swim on the same day you do one of the shorter workouts in one of the other sports. However, you can certainly distribute the six workouts over six days if you wish.

You can determine for yourself the best distribution of the three sports within your scheduled workout. I generally swim once a week, run twice, and bike three times, primarily because cycling happens to be my favorite sport of the three. You can decide what you think will work best for you, but you should swim a minimum of once a week and both bike and run a minimum of twice a week. Once you get into the sport, you can vary the distributions from one thirteen-week block to the next, as your experience indicates.

The program begins at 290 minutes for the first week and builds up to 350 minutes in the fifth. The sixth and seventh weeks total 155 and 205 minutes respectively, with just five workouts each week. Following the Bill Bowerman hard/easy principle overall, the program gives you a chance to consolidate your gains here. You then do 390, 395, 465, and 390 again in weeks eight through eleven.

Included are workouts of 100 and 150 minutes. In these workouts I suggest you combine bike and run segments, to get a bit of the two-sport flavor before you do that first race. (In the triathlon vernacular, a combined bike/run workout is called a "brick.") You can certainly add one or two longer workouts if you wish to, but they aren't necessary. You'll taper in the twelfth and thirteenth weeks with 220 and 60 minutes, respectively.

TABLE 3-2		The Standard-distance Triathlon Training Program						
Day:	M	T	W	Th	F	S	S	Total
WEEK			(TIMES	IN	MINUTES)			
1	Off	40/35	45	Off	45	65	60	290
2	Off	40/40	50	Off	45	70	65	310
3	Off	45/40	55	Off	50	75	70	335
4	Off	45/45	50	Off	55	75	65	335
5	Off	50/45	55	Off	65	75	60	350
6	Off	40	30	Off	25	35	25	155
7	Off	30	40	Off	35	45	55	205
8	Off	55/50	70	Off	65	80	70	390
9	Off	55/50	60	Off	65	90	75	395
10	Off	65/60	75	Off	75	90	100*	465
11	Off	45/45	50	Off	55	45	150*	390
12	Off	45	Off	60	Off	70	45	220
13	Off	20	20	20	20	RACE		

*These two workouts should be two combination bike/runs or walks ("bricks"), so you can get some experience changing your clothing and doing two sports consecutively.

These numbers average out to five hours per week for thirteen weeks. In my own season, once I've completed the Standard-distance program (and I've used it faithfully every year I've been triathloning myself), I generally repeat the week-eight-through-week-eleven schedule. If I happen to be racing in any of those weeks, I count my race times toward my training totals. That schedule, using weeks eight to eleven, averages out to close to seven hours per week. You can certainly lower that total (including race times) to six hours and stay in good trim for the racing season.

Duathlon Adjustments

If you're training for a duathlon rather than a triathlon, obviously you won't be doing any swimming. Nor will you need as much total time as you would for a triathlon. Assuming the race is a Standard-course duathlon, in the neighborhood of a 3-mile run/18-mile bike/3-mile run, simply drop the second Tuesday workout in each of the nine weeks for which it's scheduled. You could also reduce the two long combined bike/run workouts to 90 and 120 minutes from 100 and 150. At the end of thirteen weeks on this program, you'll still be well trained for a Standard-course duathlon.

WHERE THE TRAINING PROGRAMS COME FROM

*T*he Standard-distance program has worked for me and many other triathletes season after season. Over the years, many a triathlete has come up to me at a race to tell me that my original program—in my book *Triathloning for Ordinary Mortals*, on which the ETTP is based—had worked for them. For example, I recall one particular first-time participant in the 1987 Seaside Triathlon (Hyannis, MA) who told me how helpful he had found my training program. This might not have been notable except that he passed on this information *during* the race—as he slowly passed me on the run leg. "Why did I have to be *so* helpful," I thought at the time.

Several years ago triathlete Larry Kaiser of Cape Cod, Massachusetts, wrote to me that "I have always believed training should fill in the spare time of our days rather than consume our entire day or take time away from other important activities such as friends, family, work, other hobbies and relaxation." I couldn't agree more.

For persons doing a Standard-distance triathlon just about every weekend during the season, Larry suggested a training program of one session per week in each sport at the Standard distances, that is, one 1.5k swim, one 40k bike, one 10k run. That's about three hours per week of training with a race/workout of about three hours each weekend, for a total of six hours. That sounds good to me. It should work well for the frequent racer and be fun, too.

The Standard-distance triathlon is the time/distance equivalent of something less than running a marathon, in the neighborhood of a 20-mile run. There are several well-respected "first marathon" programs, in use since the '70s, that average about five hours per week for thirteen weeks or so. That's the base from which I developed the original version of the ETTP, now modified by further experience.

At the time when I was planning to do my first triathlon, two of the then-prominent training programs for first-time marathoners were to be found in Ardy Friedberg's *How to Run Your First Marathon* (1982) and Joe Henderson's *Jog, Run, Race* (1977). After recommending the establishment of a base two and a half to three hours per week for three months or so, Ardy's program called for about four hours per week for thirteen weeks leading up to the marathon, Joe's for about six. I settled on five hours a week. In that neighborhood, too, is Jeff Galloway's marathon-training program featured in the companion to this book, *The Essential Marathoner* by John Hanc (1996).

CONCERNING SPEED

*R*emember that speed is not just the result of how much training you do. But neither is it entirely preordained. Your performance in a given race is the product of *both* training and innate ability. Some people are naturally fast and can do "well" in terms of finish-place without training too much. If they trained more, they could go even faster. But they're happy to not train much and to simply go out there and enjoy themselves. Even though they are fast relative to many of their fellow triathletes, they are, in their heads, recreational triathletes. They *know* inside that they *could* go faster, but choose not to do the training that going faster would necessitate.

The same applies to slow folks. If you're naturally slow, you can increase your speed to some extent by training harder. I'm slow and I accept my built-in slowness and choose to just get out there and enjoy myself rather than worry about my speed. And if, on a given day, I happen to go a little faster than expected, that's nice, too. Icing on the cake. But whether you're naturally fast or naturally slow, if you'd like to train for speed, you're best advised to use a program. For running, you might consult Bob Glover and Pete Schuder's *The Competitive Runner's Handbook* (1988). For cycling, consider *Smart Cycling* by Dr. Arnie Baker (1994).

AEROBIC TRAINING

*Y*ou've probably heard a lot about "aerobic exercise," or exercise intense enough to lead to a *significant* increase in the use of breathed-in oxygen by the muscles. Exercise that is not so intense as to cause a significant increase in the use of breathed-in oxygen by the muscles is "nonaerobic." ("Anaerobic exercise," by the way, is intense, short-term exercise fueled not by breathed-in oxygen but by energy sources within your muscles.) Certainly, if you're planning to *race* with your heart rate in your aerobic range, you'll need to *train* with your heart rate in your aerobic range*.

How do you know if you're exercising aerobically? Many triathletes who are competing to win or place within their age group, and who perform well in those terms, both train and race using a heart-rate monitor that tells them just what their heart rate is. They need to get their heart rate well up into their aerobic range—how to find out just what your aerobic range is will be covered shortly—in each of the three events. The monitor will tell them if they're pushing themselves at their most efficient pace at that particular time (see chapter 6 for information on heart monitors). Another way of determining your heart rate is by taking your pulse.

Taking Your Pulse

We can't walk (or run or bike) around with little me-

---

*There is nothing written anywhere that says that if you're racing you *have* to be working out at an aerobic level of intensity. When you race at a subaerobic level, you're certainly not going to race competitively, but that doesn't mean you can't be there and have fun. I know—from how I feel or from very occasionally taking my pulse or using a heart-rate monitor just for the fun of it—that often in both my workouts and my races, my heart rate is either not up in my aerobic range or at the low end of it. But I don't primarily train my heart to go fast: I train my body and my mind to go long. And I can do that without making my heart go too fast. I'm out there to have a good time. If on a particular day that means that I'll be going fast enough to get my heart rate up, fine. Nevertheless, I fully endorse aerobic exercise. It has more long-term health benefits than nonaerobic exercise. And, as I previously noted, if winning or placing in your age group is what you want, that's going to be hard to do without training and racing aerobically.

The Essential Triathlete

ters that tell us what our muscles are doing in the way of oxygen use at any given time. But our heart rate provides a good and simple measure of whether or not exercise is aerobic. To determine your heart rate, you can buy a heart-rate monitor. Or, much more cheaply, you can take your own pulse.

You can do this at your wrist, but there's a much easier way. On the side of your neck there's a thick band of muscle that runs from the angle at the back of your lower jaw to the notch that marks the middle of your collarbone. On one side of your neck, feel with the index and middle fingers of your opposite-side hand along the front border of this muscle band. About halfway down, you'll come across the carotid artery, a large, pulsating blood vessel. You should be able to locate one carotid or the other fairly easily.

Caution: DO NOT DO THIS ON BOTH SIDES OF YOUR NECK SIMULTANEOUSLY. YOU COULD CAUSE YOURSELF TO PASS OUT, OR WORSE. Also, do not use this method if you have any suspicion that you might have carotid artery disease on even one side.

Once you've found your pulse, you can determine your heart rate with either a digital watch or one with a sweep second hand. Count the number of beats for six seconds. Multiply by ten and you have your heart rate per minute. That's all there is to it.

Various formulas have been developed for telling us whether a given heart rate means we're exercising at an aerobic level of intensity. A simple one goes as follows. First, subtract your age from the number 220. The resulting number is called the "theoretical" maximum heart rate, which is the approximate rate above which your heart simply cannot beat without sustaining damage in some way. Sixty percent of your theoretical maximum is now considered to be the minimum Target Heart Rate

(THR) you need to reach to be sure that the exercise you're doing is aerobic. Table 3-3 shows the minimum THR for some sample ages. To be on the safe side, you should never exercise so hard that your heart rate goes above 80 percent of your theoretical max. Thus the safe "Target Zone" is 60 to 80 percent of the number 220 minus your age.

There are more sophisticated formulas available. For example, Dr. Philip Maffetone, coach and trainer for many top professional triathletes, recommends the "180

TABLE 3-3	Minimum Aerobic Heart Rates for Selected Ages

(60 Percent of Theoretical Maximum Heart Rate)

Age	Heart Rate
21	119
25	117
30	114
35	111
39	109
40	108
45	105
50	102
55	99
60	96
65	93
70	90
75	87
80	84
85	81
90	78

Formula" (1994). It produces one number for a recommended heart rate that, among other things, will likely reflect a level of muscle oxygen-uptake that will lead to maximum body fat-burning for energy.

With this formula, you first subtract your age from the number 180. Then, in addition: If you're recovering from a major illness or are on one or more major medications regularly, subtract 10; if you're starting from scratch, coming back from injury, or suffer frequently from colds or allergies, subtract 5; if you've been working out aerobically for two years or less and are healthy, use the number as is; if you've been working out aerobically for two years or more, are healthy, and are getting faster/longer, add 5. If you're unsure which of two categories you're in, choose the more conservative one. To arrive at a range for your workouts, subtract 10 from whatever your "180 Formula" number is.

Unmodified, this formula produces a number generally in the range of 75 to 80 percent of the "theoretical maximum heart rate" standard (220 minus your age). The 180 Formula is more suited to multisport athletes aiming toward their eventual maximum potential. I find the range of 60 to 65 percent of 220-minus-my-age to be quite a comfortable zone for my workouts, most of the time. And I do get where I want to go, at a speed I'm happy with in most of my races, as you know by now.

Qualitative measures of exercise intensity are perhaps as useful as heart-rate monitoring. If you're breathing reasonably hard, and/or sweating while working out in mild to cold temperatures, you can usually assume that you're exercising aerobically. There's also the "talk test." If you can carry on a conversation with a partner (or yourself) while working out, you are, at least, not going *too* fast. At the top end, however, monitoring your pulse is a good idea.

WARMING UP
AND STRETCHING

*T*his is a somewhat controversial area (Lewand-owski, 1995). Virtually all exercise authorities recommend some kind of warm-up period in each session before you go full throttle (whatever "full throttle" happens to mean for you), and some kind of cool-down at the end of it. A minimum of 5 to 10 minutes of warm-up and 3 to 5 minutes of cool-down is a good idea. Once you're above 20 minutes per workout, whether or not you count those minutes as part of the scheduled time for that session is entirely up to you.

Many authorities believe that stretching your muscles before you begin exercising makes you much less susceptible to injury while you're doing it. However, not all exercise authorities recommend a specific program of stretching, and a few even recommend against it. I have to admit that while I warm up and cool down before and after working out, I rarely go through a formal set of stretches before or after workouts, although I do usually incorporate a 5-to-10–minute session of stretching in my off-season winter workouts. While I'm obviously not a stickler on the subject, I believe that stretching before each workout is useful for many people.

*Before You Exercise**

For 5 to 10 minutes you gently warm up at least a bit *before* stretching because warmer muscles can be stretched

---

*This chapter section is based on the sections of my book *Regular Exercise: A Handbook for Clinical Practice* (1995) entitled "Before You Exercise" and "Stretching Exercises" (pp. 136–138), sections that were in turn based on the work of F. Skip Latella (Latella and Conklin, 1989).

more easily without risk of pulls or tears than colder ones can. This will increase the blood circulation to your muscles. Start your warm-up exercise of choice (for example, jogging, walking, or riding a stationary bicycle) at a slow to moderate pace.

A recommended series of slow, static stretches is presented below. At the end of each stretch, you should hold the muscle in an extended position for 10 to 30 seconds. As you stretch each muscle, you will gradually feel a resistance developing in it, like the tension you feel in a rubber band as you stretch it. Continue your stretch until you feel a slight pull, but never to the point of feeling pain. Don't bounce. Bouncing can cause muscle tears. Breathe slowly and steadily. Most people find it comfortable to inhale through the nose, exhale through the mouth.

Cooling Down

Toward the end of your workout, always give your body a chance to recover a bit and then cool down gradually. First, continue the activity you've been doing, but at a slower pace, for 2 to 3 minutes. Many authorities recommend that you then stretch for a few minutes, even if you did so at the beginning of your workout. The more you stretch during cool-down, the less likely you are to feel the effects of exercise the next day. This approach can help prevent post-workout dizziness, fainting, vomiting, and muscle soreness.

Stretching Exercises

The following stretching exercises can be used in both the warm-up and cool-down periods. You may not be able to perform all of them comfortably, at least not in the beginning. Pick ones that you like and that are related to the sport/activity you're doing. Remember that the aphorism "gradual change leads to permanent changes" applies to stretching as well as to other parts of your exercise program. And again, remember to stretch, not bounce.

NECK STRETCH.   Stand tall with your back straight, and relax your shoulders. Tilt your head to the right, to the rear, to the left, and then forward. Hold each position 10 seconds, and repeat five to ten times in each direction. Don't roll your neck, but gently stretch it in each direction.

SHOULDER STRETCH. Stand tall, with your shoulders relaxed. Stretch your arms behind your back and clasp your hands. Lift your arms behind you until you feel a stretch in your arms, chest, and shoulders. Keep your shoulders down and as relaxed as possible. Hold one time for 30 seconds.

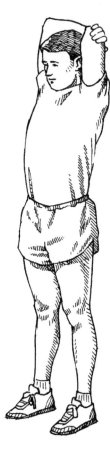

TRICEPS STRETCH. The triceps is the muscle on the underside of your upper arm. Reach your left arm up and behind you as if to scratch your left shoulder blade. Place your right hand on your left elbow and gently pull it backward to extend the stretch. Hold one time for 30 seconds. Repeat with the right arm.

HAMSTRING STRETCH. The term "hamstrings" refers to the muscles on the back of your thigh. Sit on the floor with your left leg straight out in front of you and your right leg tucked against your right thigh, close to the body. If your hamstrings hurt in this position, bend your knee enough to relieve the pain. Reach for the ankle of your left leg. Bend forward from your hips while keeping your back straight. Don't bounce. Hold one time for 30 seconds, then repeat with the opposite leg.

MODIFIED HAMSTRING STRETCH. Stand with your left leg resting on the seat of a chair or on a low counter. Keep your right leg slightly bent. Reach for the ankle of your extended leg (taking the same precautions as for the hamstring stretch). Bend forward from your hips and keep your back straight. Hold one time for 30 seconds, then repeat with the opposite leg.

GROIN STRETCH.   Sit on the floor, with the soles of your feet pressed together. Hold your ankles, and with your elbows placed on your knees, press down gently. Keep your back straight. Hold one time for 30 seconds.

FULL-BODY STRETCH.   Lie flat on your back on the floor, with your arms extended over your head. Stretch your arms and legs, lengthening your arms, shoulders, rib cage, abdominals, spine, legs, and feet. Breathe slowly and steadily. Hold one time for 30 seconds.

MODIFIED QUADRICEPS STRETCH. The quadriceps are the muscles on the front of your thigh. Stand tall and hold a chair-back or counter to help you keep your balance. Slowly bend your knees. Keep your back straight and your weight over your pelvis. Hold one time for 30 seconds. (This exercise is not actually a stretch, but a mild contraction of the muscle fibers. Nevertheless, it warms up the muscle and may improve flexibility.)

CALF STRETCH. Stand about an arm's distance from a wall. With both hands on the wall and both arms slightly bent, bend your left knee and stretch your right leg behind you. Keep your right leg straight, with your foot flat on the floor and your toes pointed straight ahead. Keep your back straight and aligned with the extended leg. Lean forward to feel a stretch along your calf muscle. Hold one time for 30 seconds. Repeat with the opposite leg.

HEALTHY EATING

*H*ealthy eating will considerably help you make your training successful and your racing a happy experience. The well-known sports nutritionist Nancy Clark uses three terms to characterize healthy eating: variety, moderation, and wholesomeness. Variety means, of course, eating different foods so that you don't get bored. And there is as much variety among healthy foods as there is among fat-laden, unhealthy ones.

Moderation, too, means just what it says. In practice that means a few simple things: eating at least three meals a day, not two or one; making sure to eat a breakfast with good nutritional value, including fruit and fiber; when you feel hungry between meals, eating a healthy snack such as fruit—fresh or dried—some crunchy veggies, a low-fat granola bar, or a few fig bars; and learning *not* to eat anything more once you experience that full feeling while having a meal (even if that means incurring the wrath of your mother by resigning from the clean-plate club).

What is healthy food? Most people today know what that means: food high in carbohydrates, low in fat, moderate in protein. Specifically, carbohydrates include: pasta (without fatty sauces), whole-grain breads, rice, potatoes (without a lot of high-fat toppings), crackers, cereals, bagels, and fruits and vegetables.

Does "low in fat" mean you should eat *no* fat? No. It does mean perhaps eating less meat than you may be accustomed to; choosing lower-fat varieties of meat like flank steak, or substituting chicken (without the skin) or fish; cutting down on the cheese and/or choosing low-fat varieties; choosing a type of milk that's lower in fat; and going for sherbet (sorbet) or low- or no-fat yogurt rather than ice cream. And "moderate" protein means just that, moderate. In addition to lean meat, chicken, and fish, the legumes, beans, peas, and lentils are an excellent source of protein (and are naturally fat-free).

Furthermore, none of this means *never* eating rich, very fatty foods. It just means doing so only on occasion. Moderation does mean moderation, not elimination. Interestingly enough, many people find that if they limit their intake of rich food, their taste for it diminishes.

HEALTHY EATING OVER TIME. Healthy eating begins in the supermarket and continues in the kitchen. You can't maintain a healthy diet if you don't supply yourself with healthy foods. You can't eat unhealthy foods, at home at least, unless you bring them into the house. And in preparing food, it's important to learn how to cook without using fat and how to prepare food—like meat—in such a way as to minimize the amount of fat that remains in it after cooking.

Also, you can prepare vegetables so that they're limp, lifeless, and completely unappetizing, or you can prepare them so that they're colorful, crunchy, and great-tasting. There's a variety of low-fat cookbooks available in your local bookstore to help you prepare inherently nutritious foods in the most healthy and appetizing ways (see the appendix).

Healthy eating is a lifelong project. It's not a regimen that you follow for a fixed period of time and then abandon. Such a pattern won't be effective; you'll not only miss out on the benefits of good nutrition, but your body and sense of taste will never adapt to healthy eating if you keep supplying them with unhealthy food.

If you want to eat a healthier diet, don't try to change your unhealthy patterns all at once. Just as with exercise: gradual change leads to permanent changes.

ON WEIGHT LOSS. The key to successful weight loss, if it's in the cards for you, is not dieting. It is establishing a pattern of healthy eating and regular exercise—like the one we're talking about in this book—that you'll be able to stick with for the rest of your life.

Successful weight loss is a slow process. Patience is the key. Losing one pound a week is a healthy way to do it.

Finally—although this is a somewhat controversial point—it appears that some regular exercisers in very good physical condition do not and perhaps cannot lose weight on a high-carbohydrate/low-fat diet. Why not? you might ask.

Since the hormone insulin (in addition to mobilizing blood sugar) keeps fat stored within the cells, thus preventing it from being available for use as fuel, the problem may have something to do with insulin metabolism in the well-conditioned person. Some regular exercisers (myself included) have had success in losing weight eating a moderate-carbohydrate, moderate-protein, moderate-fat diet while maintaining a full exercise schedule of the type outlined in this book.

With this moderate eating pattern, the fat intake is still at a heart-healthy 30-percent-of-calories-in-fat level, but it's not down at the 10 to 15-percent level of many low-fat eating programs. (Protein intake is about at the 30-percent level as well.) If you're a regular exerciser out to lose some weight, and you find that high carbs/low fat doesn't work for you, you might want to try some variant of this approach, commonly referred to as the "40-30-30" plan.

SUPPLEMENTS. If you eat a healthy, balanced diet with plenty of fruits and vegetables, you don't have to take a vitamin supplement unless you have a specific, measured vitamin deficiency. However, unless you have a specific vitamin-intolerance (which is very rare), or are, for example, a pregnant woman who should be certain to keep Vitamin A intake very modest, taking a daily vitamin-supplement capsule won't hurt you, and you'll be covering your bases just in case what you eat doesn't happen to fully supply your needs.

FLUIDS. If you're a regular exerciser, you should make sure to maintain your body-fluid level regularly, not just when you're working out. And when you are working out, make sure that you drink adequately, *before* you feel thirsty (by the time you become thirsty it's too late to catch up as long as you continue to exercise). The fluid of choice? The choice is yours. Just before and during exercise, there's no evidence that—although they are a ready source of calories—any of the advertised sports drinks adds anything *special* to one's energy level or stamina. But if you like the flavor of one or another of them, and would rather get a caloric boost in liquid than solid form, fine. As for me, I prefer water.

SPORTS BARS. The so-called "sports bars" have become very popular in recent years (Clark, 1995). They come in two varieties of nutrient combinations: high carbohydrates with low fats and proteins, or each nutrient in moderation, the so-called "40-30-30" bar. Both are useful for providing an easily digestible energy supply both before and during exercise sessions. In chapter 7 I note that after trying many different combinations of foods over many years, my prerace "meal," one that I'm very happy with, consists of one energy bar upon arising and another about half an hour before the race.

The 40-30-30 bars may be useful in a weight-loss program for well-conditioned athletes because of their apparent effect on moderating insulin release, thus enabling the easier mobilization and use of body fat for energy. (I myself have found that such a program works.) But if you're simply using a high-carbohydrate bar to supply you with readily available energy during a workout or a race, check out the low-fat granola bars. They'll give you the same amount of carbs and calories as one of the brand-name high-carb bars for one-third to one-fifth the cost.

One *caveat:* Even though most of the brand-name energy bars are supplemented with vitamins and minerals, do not be tempted to use them as meal substitutes. You won't be eating a balanced diet and, if you're exercising, you'll be eating too few calories, a situation that can lead perhaps to short-term weight loss but also possibly to long-term metabolism imbalance.

IN THE OFF-SEASON

*L*et's finish up this chapter with some thoughts on winter or other off-season activities. First of all, I believe that everyone should take some downtime, some absolute rest, no training at all. A week, two weeks, even a month if you've done a lot of racing in the past season, or perhaps had an injury or two that could use some plain old rest to help the healing process. As noted, if you're in good shape, you won't lose too much of your conditioning even with extended rest. Many studies that show rapid loss of conditioning in the absence of training were done on people who had just gotten into shape. Research on well-conditioned athletes has shown that there's little harm in taking some downtime. The potential benefits of recharging the mind and the body are great.

Some of the "positively addicted" endurance athletes among us may find it hard to stop or stop completely. Irritability when not training regularly is a common complaint. If you count yourself among that group, then at least cut back.

Second, during the winter season think about your goals in triathlon. What goals did you set for the past season? Were they reasonable ones for you? Did you have the mind-set, the body conditioning, and the time availability such that they were realistic? Did you achieve your goals? If you did, did you feel good about it, did the effort work for you, or did you give up too much in other parts of your life and/or get injured in the process?

If you didn't reach your goals or did but didn't feel good, why not? Were the goals you set unrealistic? Did other things happen during the season that got in the way? How did you feel about that? How does your goal setting affect your feelings about your achievements or lack thereof?

I don't always achieve all of my goals during a season, even if they were reasonable ones for me. For example, back in 1988, I had planned to do seven to eight races. Because of a late-season ski injury and an unexpectedly busy summer at work, I ended up doing four. I don't set my goals rigidly. They are rather "hope-fors" and "strive-fors." They define ranges, not requirements of performance for me. Whatever level you're at (unless you have to earn a living from the sport), I suggest that approach. It's especially good for the recreational triathlete. As I've noted more than once, this sport should produce happiness, not pain. How you frame your goals can have a great deal of influence on both the mental and physical outcomes for you.

The off-season is also the time to start thinking about your goals for next season. Do you want to do more races? Fewer? Do you want to do longer ones? Shorter ones? Do you want to try to go faster? Is it perhaps time to take a sabbatical? After I'd been racing for six years, I gave some thought to taking the seventh year off to do something else. Perhaps the time had come, I thought, to learn how to play tennis, or to get back into sailing. In the end, I was back at triathloning that next season. But I did think about it. Whatever you do set as goals, make sure that they're realistic ones.

For my own winter training, I've developed a program that involves a bit of weight training, some regular stretching, swimming, indoor biking, occasional running (on cool, crisp, clear days), some downhill skiing. I use the Maintenance program, working out for a total of about three hours per week. It keeps me fit, it keeps me sharp, but it doesn't wear me out over the winter. Come spring, I'm ready and raring to go outdoors once again.

TABLE 3-4								

The Maintenance Triathlon Training Program
(Averaging Three Hours per Week; Times in Minutes)

Day:	M	T	W	Th	F	S	S	Total
WEEK			(TIMES IN MINUTES)					
1	Off	30	Off	40	Off	30	50	150
2	Off	40	Off	30	Off	40	60	170
3	Off	30	Off	50	Off	40	60	180
4	Off	40	Off	50	Off	40	60	190
5	Off	30	Off	50	Off	40	60	180
6	Off	40	Off	30	Off	40	60	170
7	Off	40	Off	40	Off	40	60	180
8	Off	40	Off	40	Off	50	70	200
9	Off	40	Off	50	Off	40	60	190
10	Off	30	Off	50	Off	40	50	170
11	Off	40	Off	30	Off	50	70	190
12	Off	40	Off	30	Off	40	70	180
13	Off	40	Off	50	Off	40	60	180

REFERENCES

American College of Sports Medicine (ACSM). *ACSM Fitness Book*. Champaign, IL: Leisure Press, 1992.

Baker, A. *Smart Cycling*. San Diego, CA: Argo Publishing, 1994.

Clark, N. "Energy Bars." In *The Physician and Sports Medicine*, Vol. 23, No. 9, 1995, p. 7.

Friedberg, A. *How to Run Your First Marathon*. New York: Fireside/Simon & Schuster, 1982.

Glover, B., and P. Schuder. *The Competitive Runner's Handbook*. New York: Viking Penguin, 1988.

Hanc, J. *The Essential Marathoner*. New York: Lyons & Burford, 1996.

Hanc, J. *The Essential Runner*. New York: Lyons & Burford, 1994.

Henderson, J. *Jog, Run, Race*. Mountain View, CA: World Publications, 1977.

Jonas, S., and the Editors of Consumer Reports Books. *Take Control of Your Weight*. Yonkers, NY: Consumer Reports Books, 1993.

Latella, F. S., W. Conkling, and the Editors of Consumer Reports Books. *Get in Shape, Stay in Shape*. Yonkers, NY: Consumer Reports Books, 1989.

Lewandowski, P. "To Stretch or Not to Stretch?" In *Triathlete*, June 1995, p. 106.

Maffetone, P. "Heart Rate Monitoring and the New 180 Formula." In *Triathlete*, November 1994, p. 10.

Walsh, C. *The Bowerman System*. Los Altos, CA: Tafnews Press, 1983.

4

CHOOSING
YOUR RACES

If you're a first-time tri- or duathlete, even before you begin your ETTP you should be thinking about the choice you'll make for your first race. The information presented in this chapter will help you to make that choice a sensible one for you. If you're already a recreational triathlete, but have approached your racing and race selection somewhat haphazardly, you'll probably find the information in this chapter to be helpful as well.

Especially for first-timers, race scheduling is important. You want to make sure that you'll have enough time to get in the requisite training before you find yourself at a starting line for the first time. As you know by now, if you're starting from scratch, you'll need about six months to get in all of your training .

Among the race characteristics to consider when making your choice(s) are:

- race types and lengths
- distance of the race(s) from home
- convenience
- availability of overnight accommodations (if necessary)
- registration procedures
- course and transition-area characteristics
- type of water for the swim (fresh or salt)
- swim location (pool/lake/protected salt water/open ocean)
- water temperature
- hills
- heat
- shade
- road surface
- traffic
- logistic support
- spectator opportunities
- parking

TYPES OF RACES

The Common Triathlon

The three legs of most triathlons are swimming, cycling, and running, done in that order. There are good reasons why the order is the way it is. The swim is potentially the most dangerous of the three events (although serious injuries rarely occur in any of them). Thus it's advantageous to have the racers swim when they're at their freshest. Furthermore, there's almost always a wide range of swimming ability among triathletes, so the field gets spread out.

This is an advantage for race logistics when it comes to the bike leg. There will less likely be bike traffic-jams on the (often narrow) roads on which most triathlon bike races are held. And there will be less likelihood that large numbers of competitors will be close enough to each other to be tempted to engage in "drafting" (riding close behind a cyclist just in front of you, to cut down on wind resistance), a practice that is intrinsic to bicycle racing but against the rules in most triathlons.

Most duathlons also have three legs: run/bike/run, although some are just run/bike. But almost invariably a run is the first event in a duathlon, serving to spread out the field—just as the swim does in a triathlon, and for the same reasons.

The Uncommon

There are some multisport events that have other combinations of sports. While you might not choose one of them for your first go, once you get into multisport racing you might consider doing one every now and then. In 1992, I did a Memorial Day–weekend race at Killington, Vermont, that involved downhill skiing (on a steep trail with huge bumps), mountain biking, and cross-country running. There are other varieties of triathlon (or even quad- or quintathlons) that include, for example, one or more of: cross-country skiing, snowshoeing, canoeing, kayaking, and rowing. But it's likely that you'll choose a conventional combination for your first race, and I advise that course of action.

LENGTH

As for length, in triathlon you can start with either a Standard-distance triathlon (1.5k [0.93-mile] swim/40k [24.8-mile] bike/10k [6.2-mile] run), or a Sprint (in the range of a ¼-to-½–mile swim/10-to-15–mile bike/3-to-5–mile run), or you can start off with a duathlon. Pick the type of race and distance you feel most comfortable with. Many people enter the sport with a Sprint or a duathlon. If you find that you like multisport racing, there will be plenty of opportunities to do longer races in the future. Don't be afraid of starting out with a shorter one. Doing a Sprint triathlon or two to get started in the sport is a very good way to learn about the sport's logistics. Without having a big, big race taking up a lot of your mind space, you can focus more on practical matters, like gathering together the equipment you need for three sports, making sure that it all gets into the car, and efficiently organizing the stuff in the transition area.

The Sprint distance can be fine fun and a real challenge for the experienced triathlete as well. It's a great way to stay in shape and to focus on aspects of your racing other than endurance. Speed in transitions and the time in which you finish each leg become more important in a Sprint than in a longer race. In my seventh season of triathlon, with two ironman-distance, several half-ironman, a bunch of Standard-distance, and occasional shorter races under my belt, I decided to try the Sprint distance as a major feature of my season. I did three of them and had a great time at it.

As you know by now, I am slow. So I'm slow in the shorter races as well as in the longer ones. But in a Sprint, if you're in any kind of decent shape at all you can "hammer" it all the way through. So just like the fast folks who do the Sprints, I was able to hammer—at my own hammering pace, to be sure. If you're used to doing longer distances, you know that you'll be able to get out there in a Sprint and push hard for the whole race without worrying about wearing out or hitting the wall. It's really fun just to try to go as fast as *you* can go for the whole thing.

RULES

*T*he rules for triathlon and duathlon racing, used in almost all competitions, are the ones established by the USA Triathlon (see the appendix). While there are quite a few rules concerning the technical conduct of the race itself that may be of concern to fast racers competing for awards, there are only a few rules that need to be of concern to most of us.

SWIMMING.   Any stroke is permissible. You may stand on the bottom, if you can reach it, and if you want to use it to help your forward motion, you can. (But if on entering or exiting the swim you try to walk in shallow water, you'll go more slowly than if you were swimming.) Resting (without trying to move forward) on an inanimate object, such as a lifeguard's board, is permissible (and encouraged if you're tired). Wetsuit use is permitted in almost any conditions (if it's not permitted in a particular race, the whys and wherefores will be announced). You must wear a cap (usually, but not always, supplied). Swim goggles are permitted, but not required.

CYCLING.   Almost any kind of upright bike is permitted. (Recumbents are prohibited, as are a few really weird types of bikes that the recreational multisport athlete would hardly consider using.) You must ride the bike in the race. Unless the bike is mechanically disabled, you cannot walk it through any part of the course other than the transition area. Helmets, with chin straps secured while riding, are required. Drafting—riding close enough behind a rider in front of you to take advantage of the windbreak created by that rider's forward motion—is prohibited in most triathlons.

RUNNING. Any style of running or walking is permitted. Headsets are prohibited. You may carry a water bottle and/or a fanny pack.

TRANSITION AREA. You must follow all instructions given to competitors by race officials regarding transition-area bike and equipment placement, occupancy (noncompetitors are generally excluded), and conduct.

DISTANCE FROM HOME

*F*or openers, it's usually a good idea to choose a race that's reasonably close to home. That way, you can sleep in your own bed the night before without having to get up at an overwhelmingly punishing early hour in order to get to the starting line on time.

Let's say that the start time is 8:00 A.M. You should allow yourself at least one hour at the race site to check in, organize your stuff, attend to bodily functions, and so forth. Actually, and especially for that first race, allowing an hour and a half is an even better idea. That means you'll probably want to find a race within an hour's driving time of your home. Then, if it takes you an hour or so to get up and out of the house (as it does me), you'll need to arise no earlier than 4:30 A.M., preferably closer to 5:00.

On the other hand, you may find it more convenient to stay right in the race neighborhood the night before. Once you get into the sport, you'll probably want to travel around a bit, just for the variety and adventure. You can often get lists of local accommodations from the race director. If not, these places can be found through the chamber of commerce for the race locality or an automobile club.

If you do need to stay overnight, it's a good idea to book your reservations as early as possible, because the hotels/motels close by, with reasonable rates, tend to fill up first, and not all races are held in areas that feature large numbers of lodgings. Since you'll have a bike with you, you'll be better served by a motel than a hotel. Of the former, the most convenient are the ones with direct entry to the room from the parking area, on the first floor, of course.

If you get ambitious, you may decide to fly to a race in another part of the country. That's a grand adventure to be sure, but it's not cheap. On top of the usual costs of distant travel, you'll need to buy or rent a bike carrying-case for the plane (some local bike dealers have this item available for rent; see also chapter 6). You'll *never* want to ship your bike on a plane just in a corrugated bike box. The risk of damage is just too high. Unless you belong to an organization like US Amateur (see the appendix), which provides for free bike carriage on certain airlines, you'll pay an extra fee for transporting your bike.

At the race locale, you'll need to rent a car (usually a station wagon) or a van into which you can fit your encased bike. You may not have the opportunity to scope out the race course in advance, as you can do with a course within reasonable driving distance of your home. You'll need to learn how to pack and reassemble your bike (allow plenty of time for that).

DATE

*I*f at all possible, you should pick the date of your first race so that you won't have to begin your training in cold, possibly snowy weather. At the same, it's advisable to do that first one on a day that will likely not be overwhelmingly hot. Thus, in most parts of the United States and Canada, June (if you're ready to go right into the Standard-distance Triathlon Training Program) and September (if you need to do the Foundation program first) are good months for your triathlon/duathlon racing debut. In the South and Southwest you might want to, and be able comfortably to, go earlier or later in the year.

RACE REGISTRATION

*R*ace registration means filling out a race application, signing a liability waiver, and paying the entry fee. Fees range from $20 to $100, but for most Sprints, Standard-distance tri's, and duathlons, fees are in the $30 to $45 range (as of 1995). For many triathlons, you'll need to register through the mail before the race. For some races, especially the longer and/or heavily attended ones, you're required to check in to confirm your participation and pick up your race numbers the day before the race. However, some races do have morning-of-the-race registration (usually at a higher cost than for prerace registration, and without a free T-shirt!), and most have morning-of-the-race check-in. You can find out the details by calling or writing the race director.

You can find schedules of races in one or more of the sources in "Where to Find Races Listed," (page 103). Both when sending for race information and when sending in the race-registration application, be sure to enclose a self-addressed stamped envelope (SASE). Budgets for most triathlons and duathlons are tight, and many race directors will not respond to inquiries and/or register you for the race if an SASE is not included. As to telephoning for information, some race directors will happily and politely respond to calls. Others will not.

COURSE CHARACTERISTICS

*T*here's a variety of course characteristics to consider when making your choice of race, whether it's your first or your fiftieth. You should be comfortable with the course in your mind, so that anxiety about its nature won't compound the natural anxiety about doing the race that, regardless of the characteristics of the course, exists for most of us.

The Swim

For the swim, the first choice is whether to go in fresh water or salt water. If you haven't done much swimming, you'll probably be more comfortable in the former than the latter, even though salt water offers more buoyancy than fresh water does. A mouthful of fresh water is much easier to tolerate than an accidental gulp of salt water.

There is the occasional triathlon, such as the Central Park Triathlon in New York City, in which the swim is held in a swimming pool (outdoors and unheated in that case). But most freshwater triathlons are held in lakes. The worst condition you're likely to encounter there is a yucky bottom when entering and leaving (although many swim entrances/exits in lakes have artificial sandy bottoms).

Salt water can be found in protected bays and, of course, in open ocean. If you're going to tackle the latter (and I've done it a few times), you should be an experienced, confident swimmer, especially if you'll have to be going out through surf. In any body of salt water, you may well have to deal with surface, wind-driven waves, currents, and/or tides. Saltwater courses are usually set so that if there's a current or tide running, you'll have it going with you in one direction—even if you feel like you're swimming uphill when you go the other way.

Whatever type of water you choose, the expected temperature is a critical factor. Anything below about 69° F is going to feel cold, especially when you first get in; and the thinner you are, the colder it's going to feel. Again, for your first time, unless you own or have access to a wetsuit that fits well (see chapter 6), try to choose a race that will have a water temperature at or above 70°F. (If you're concerned, call the race director for information on this item in particular.) There will always be time to get a wetsuit and go for the colder-water races later.

The Bike

The bike-course characteristics aren't nearly as critical as the swim-course ones. But they are something to think about. Your first course route should be one that's safe, one that doesn't cross either itself or the run course. Smoothly paved, relatively lightly traveled roads are preferred, certainly. Second, the contours are important, too. You shouldn't exclude a race just because it has steep uphills; your bike should have a low-low "granny gear" for getting up hills (see chapter 6). What goes up must come down, and those downhills can be fun (except when the pavement is wet). But again, especially for the first time, it would be better for you not to encounter hills that are too long or too steep. Finally, especially if it's going to be a warm day, shade over at least a portion of the course is a nice feature.

The Run

The run-course characteristics are the least critical, because you can always walk if you have to. All the same, preferred are many of the features that characterize a good bike course: smoothly paved, relatively lightly traveled roads with a route that doesn't cross that of the bike segment; a not overly hilly layout; and some shade.

The Transition Area

Although in the early days of triathlon, having two transition areas (swim–bike and bike–run) was somewhat common, fortunately that practice has all but disappeared. The two-transition-area arrangement further complicates the already somewhat complicated logistics of multisport racing; and although they're less common, for your first race it's best to check to make sure the course you choose has only one transition area. It will also be to your advantage if there's plenty of parking nearby and only a short hike from the swim exit to the transition area. If the distance of that hike is long, be sure to stash a pair of old shoes or sandals at the exit to make that walk or trot easier. Don't worry. Not too many people do this, so you needn't anticipate searching through a mound of shoes at the end of the swim.

Competitor Support

It will help if you can be certain in advance that the

race is well organized from the check-in to the provision of after-race food to the awards ceremony; that there's an adequate number of aid stations on both bike and run courses; that traffic control is good; and that safety, in the water and on the roads, is a top priority of the race organizers. The best way to get this information is to talk with someone who has done the race before. Also, if you're bringing friends and/or family with you, you might want to check out opportunities for the spectators to view the race.

FAMILY CONSIDERATIONS

Speaking of family, you'll want to be sure, if you have a spouse or significant other, that you don't end up making that person a triathlon widow(er). If your partner also races, great. But most often that is not the case, and you'd best try to stick with the training schedule and not load up during the weekends. The way the Standard-distance program is written, there are only a few Saturdays and Sundays on which the workout sessions last much over an hour. You can pursue this sport without disappearing on the weekends. In any case, in training you are never working out for more than a couple of hours on any given day.

If you really get into the sport, try to pick most of your races so that you can reach them from home, without having to travel the day before (unless they're in really nice places that your partner would enjoy). In that way, you won't be breaking up every weekend on which you're racing.

If you're going to a race just for the day with your

partner, think about making a stop on the way home in the afternoon to do something different that you both like to do together, like visiting a museum, or hitting the local galleries and shops, or having a late lunch at a special restaurant. If you travel together for the weekend to a race away from home, plan to include some other non-racing activity, such as sight-seeing in the local area.

Watching a triathlon is not the most exciting activity in the world (even though doing it is). In few races can spectators see more than the athletes leaving and entering the transition area. And your contact with your partner during the race will usually be limited to a wave and a greeting here and there. Bringing small children to a triathlon is often not a good idea, although there are some brave souls who do it. To be successful in this endeavor, both members of the couple have to be very comfortable with the roles necessarily thrust upon them: One partner is the racer, the other primarily the caretaker for the children.

WHERE TO FIND RACES LISTED

*T*he addresses and telephone numbers of the principal sources of information such as the triathlon magazines, USA Triathlon, and the New York Triathlon Club, about the available races are listed in the appendix, "Resources."

The national triathlon/duathlon organization is called the USA Triathlon for short. For its members, the organization publishes a bimonthly newsletter called the *Triathlon Times*, which contains a calendar of USA Triathlon-sanctioned races only. (While an increasing number of races are so sanctioned by, which means that they agree to comply fully with USA Triathlon's rules and participate in its race-insurance plan, many races are not.) USA Triathlon also has available lists of regional triathlon organizations (such as the New York Triathlon Club) and regional publications and resources from which you can get information about races.

As of 1996, there were three national monthly publications for the sport: *Inside Triathlon, Triathlete,* and *220.* Each publishes national race calendars in every issue, generally organized by region and date. The listings include at least one means of contacting the race director for information and applications.

Many of the "pro" bike, running-shoe, and sporting-goods shops (see chapter 6) are staffed by people who do the sport(s) themselves. They can help, too. These will also often have applications for races being run in their local areas.

So, consult a race calendar and pick a race that's just right for you. Start your training program and stick with it. And when you finish your first race, if you're like most triathletes and duathletes, you'll want to race again and again.

TECHNIQUE

ood technique is important for each of the sports you do in triathlon or duathlon. This is true for both the relatively simple sport of long-distance running and the more complex sports of cycling and swimming. However, to be able to finish a Sprint or Standard-distance triathlon or a duathlon of the usual sort, you don't have to have *great* technique. In my view, you need not become centrally focused on technique, unless it becomes apparent that you have the potential to become competitive in multisport racing and want to do so. Becoming a technique fanatic may well take away from the fun and enjoyment of recreational

triathloning and might even get in the way of staying with it.

Regardless of your ability, *some* time devoted to technique is time well spent. Good technique makes performing each sport more comfortable and more fun. Good technique decreases muscle pain while you're engaged in an activity, as well as the risk of both intrinsic (resulting from the nature of the sport itself) and extrinsic (caused by a factor unrelated to the athletic motion) injury. It also enhances that feeling of being in control, oh so important to long-term success.

Good technique also significantly increases your athletic efficiency. Take swimming as an example. Have you ever seen someone doing the "Coney Island Crawl": head always out of the water, moving from side to side with each stroke, arms flailing away, much splash production? That person will get tired very quickly, unless he's in very, very good shape. (I once did the 2.4-mile swim of an ironman-distance triathlon behind a competitor who used the Coney Crawl all the way around the course! He *was* in very, very good shape.)

In running, landing properly on your heel helps to cushion the pounding that naturally accompanies that sport, reducing injury risk. In cycling, learning the proper use of your gears is very important, as is proper peddling cadence.

And so, let's move on to some consideration of technique for the three principal triathlon sports, not in the usual race order, but rather in the order that you'll likely approach them in your own training. After we consider running, cycling, and swimming, we'll also look at exercise-walking technique. Especially for those starting from scratch, walking can be a very useful sport in your workout program. Some people, myself included, also use it in races from time to time, and not just when we're so dog-tired on the run that we can't do anything else!

Please note that I don't hold myself out as an expert on technique in any of the sports. For expertise, you should consult one or more of the sport-specific books listed in the appendix, and even better, a coach or instructor. In my view, you can certainly refine and improve your technique by reading about it. But it's well-nigh impossible to learn from scratch a technical and, for some, intimidating sport such as swimming by reading a book.

RUNNING

*O*ne of the most popular sports for regular exercise, running is familiar to just about everyone. For most people, it's aerobic at all but the slowest speed. Running is cheap, time-efficient, and readily accessible. You can run outdoors, in most any kind of weather, and indoors too, at health clubs and gyms that have tracks—though running those short loops can become mind-numbing if you're going any distance at all—and treadmills.

People define "a runner" in different ways. Recall that Dr. George Sheehan once said that a runner is a jogger with a race entry-form. Covert Bailey, author of *The New Fit or Fat* (1991, p. 70), arbitrarily sets a maximum of an 8-minutes-per-mile pace to define running. Anything slower than that is jogging, according to Mr. Bailey. I don't know where he got the number. To my way of thinking, the best distinction is likely that found in the head of the athlete. If you think of yourself as a runner, then you are a runner, regardless of speed.

Running Safely

Running, in moderation at a reasonable pace for no more than three to four hours per week wearing shoes that fit and are in good condition, can be done over a long period of time without serious injury risk. But people sometimes forget about moderation. They run for too long at too fast a pace. Or they're careless about the fit and condition of their shoes. If they then get injured, they tend to put the blame for their injury on the sport, not themselves. That's unfortunate.

Basic running technique is simple. A former national-class hurdler once described it to me as "left, right, left, right." Well, it's not quite that simple, but that's close. In addition to left, right, it's important to keep your body relaxed, bent forward slightly from your hips (not your waist), back comfortably but not rigidly straight, head (and eyes) up, shoulders dropped, elbows comfortably bent but not locked, hands slightly below waist level, fingers lightly closed (fists not clenched), arms moving easily forward and back in rhythm with your legs.

You should try to keep your upper body quiet: no swaying from side to side or forward and back, no bouncing of the head or flailing of the arms. Extraneous upper-body motions just use energy unnecessarily and interfere with forward progress. At the other end, make sure that you bend your ankles. Ankle rigidity can lead to discomfort as easily as upper-body rigidity can.

For the foot-strike you should land on your heel, not the sole or ball of your foot. (Landing on the sole usually creates an uncomfortable slap, whereas landing on the ball for any distance at all can lead to calf-muscle strain.) After you first come down on your heel, you roll forward along the outside edge of your foot, and then

 The Essential Triathlete

▶ *Proper running form.* ◀

spring forward off the ball of your foot into the next stride. If you're making a lot of noise with each foot-strike, you're likely either landing on the sole of your foot, or leaping rather than gliding between steps. Overall, you should aim for balance, rhythm, and smoothness.

Stride Length

There's a significant variation in stride length from person to person. And you may very well discover that yours changes during the course of a workout. You'll likely take longer strides when you're going downhill, shorter ones when you're going uphill. When on level ground, you'll find that if you make your stride shorter, you will be able to move your legs faster.

Make certain not to overstride—that is, to reach too far forward with your foot. Overstriding can lead to imbalance and possible injury and can slow you down by creating a small braking action with each heel-strike. Nor will taking longer strides get you through your workout any more quickly. Since ETTP workouts are measured in minutes, not miles, you don't have to be in a hurry to get anywhere. By the same token, shorter steps won't mean a longer workout. Thus the right stride length for you is the one you're comfortable with.

CYCLING

Cycling is not only central to multisport racing, but you can also sightsee, tour, even commute on a bike. With proper technique, the risk of intrinsic injury is low. However, cycling's extrinsic-injury risk is likely the highest of any of the triathlon/duathlon sports. You have to watch out for cars and trucks, pedestrians, dogs, pot-holes, runners, and other cyclists. Attention to safety is a major consideration for any cyclist.

Top-form cycling technique is complex. It takes instruction, time, and practice to learn. To get you started safely and help you ride effectively and efficiently, here are a few simple principles that will serve you well. Once you get into the sport, you can become as high-tech a rider as you choose.

Pedaling

Most important in the realm of cycling technique is "cadence," the cyclists' term for pedal revolutions per minute (rpm). The most efficient way to bike is using a high cadence in a middling gear (see below). For beginners, that means pedaling in the 60-to-70–revolutions-per-minute range. With experience, you'll easily be able to work up your cadence to the 80-to-90–rpm range, called "spinning." Bike road-racers usually try to stay in the 90-to-105–rpm range. Many tri- or duathletes ride in the 80-to-90–rpm range, a generally comfortable one. But you might eventually find the higher, road-racing range more to your liking. Toward the end of the '95 season, after thirteen years of racing, I did so and found that I liked it. Except when going up a really steep hill on which you cannot do otherwise, pedaling in a relatively high gear, at a cadence below 50 to 60 rpm, pushing a heavy load with your legs, is inviting knee problems. You should avoid it.

You should learn how to pull up on the pedal opposite to the one you're pushing down on. This will give you more power and divide the workload between the muscles on the front of your thigh used in the push and those on the back used in the pull. Pulling up will be significantly aided if you use either bike shoes with simple cleats and toe-straps (which, however, are not recommended) or bike shoes with quick-release cleats and no straps (which are highly recommended; see next chapter). Both arrangements firmly attach your foot to the pedal so that you can pull up efficiently. But with the quick-release cleat it's much easier to disconnect from the pedal in an emergency than it is with the cleat/toe-strap system.

As with running, your upper body should be relaxed, not rigid, and as quiet as possible. This not only saves energy, it also reduces wind resistance. Further, don't scrunch up your shoulders. That can easily lead to pain across your upper back. To help absorb road shock, your elbows should be comfortably bent.

Hand Position

Many beginning cyclists ride with their hands on the "tops," the crossbar part of the handlebars. While riding that way is okay from time to time when handlebar control is not critical, the primary reason beginners do it is that the auxiliary brake handles are located there on the cheaper road bikes. Using auxiliary brake handles on a road bike is not a good idea. If your bike has them, you (or your friendly local bike mechanic) should get rid of them. Once they're gone, you'll easily become accustomed to using the main brake handles, mounted on what are called the "hoods."

Auxiliary brake handles have a soft, squishy feel. Thus, you really don't know how much brake pressure you're applying when you squeeze them. And if you have to stop suddenly, trying to decide whether to use the regular brake handles or the auxiliaries may lead to confusion. Confusion in sudden stops can lead to injury. I speak from experience. I once got confused about which brake handles to use when going into a sudden stop. I

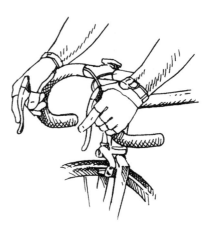

▶ *In the hoods.* ◀

ended up falling off the bike with one arm outstretched and dislocated a shoulder.

On the road bike there are two correct primary hand positions: on the brake-handle hoods and on the "drops," the lower, curved parts of the handlebars. As your speed increases on the bike, you're spending an increasing amount of your energy just moving air out of your way. Thus the lower down you get over the handlebars, the more efficiently you'll be riding.

On long rides, it's important to change hand position from time to time to avoid getting stiff. Getting a stiff neck from holding your head up so that you can see where you're going when riding on the drops is a particular problem to be avoided. Hand position on a mountain bike is simple: out on the ends of the bars, where the grips are.

Changing Gears

You change gears on a bike by altering the configuration of the chain. You'll notice that up front on both the mountain and road bikes there are two or three toothed "chainrings" mounted on a circular bracket to which the pedals are attached. Mounted on the right side of the rear wheel hub there are usually six to eight smaller toothed rings called "cogs." The particular combination of front and rear rings around which the chain is looped determines the "gear" the bike is in at any one time.

When the chain is on a large ring up front and a small one at the back, you're in a high gear. In high gear, which requires more effort, with each revolution of the pedals the wheels cover more ground than they do in a lower gear, and you go faster. Conversely, the combination of a relatively larger cog at the back and a smaller chainring up front produces a low gear. Pedaling is much easier, but you don't go as fast. The lower gears are used when going uphill, the medium ones when on the flat, and the higher ones when going downhill.

On most road bikes, the gearshift levers are mounted on the bike frame's "down tube." (That's the diagonal sloping piece that connects the handlebar tube to the pedal axle.) However, some road bikes and touring bikes might feature bar-end shifters, located at the ends of the drop handlebars. Shift levers might be mounted at the center of the handlebars on less expensive or older models. Some of the new shifting systems incorporate the shifters into the brake handles. On mountain bikes and hybrids, the shift levers are generally mounted just inboard of the hand grips, either above or below the bars, easily movable with your thumb without taking your hands off the bars. Some mountain bikes have rotating collars, called "grip shifters," on the inner portions of the hand grips to control the derailleurs.

You shift gears by moving the levers or rotating the handlebar collars. They're connected by cables to a pair of ingenious devices called "derailleurs." The derailleurs, one each for the front chainrings and the rear cog-set, are able to move the chain laterally across the respective sets of toothed rings when the pedals and rear wheel are turning.

Regardless of where they're mounted, on most bikes the left shift lever controls the derailleur for the front chainrings, the right shift lever the derailleur for the rear cogs. It will take a bit of practice to instinctively know that on the road bike, moving the left lever forward produces a lower gear while moving the right lever forward produces a higher gear, and vice versa. Actually, it might take quite a bit of practice. After thirteen years of multisport racing, from time to time I still upshift when I mean to downshift, and vice versa.

There are three important points about gearshifting that the beginner should bear in mind. First, use the left lever controlling the front chainrings if you want to make a major gear change. Use the right lever controlling the rear cogs for smaller gear adjustments. Second, when approaching a hill, be sure to drop your gear down *before* you start up. Otherwise, you may get caught in a gear that's too high for you to pedal in, and not be able to safely downshift because of pressure on the chain. Third, shift frequently. The goal is to maintain that smooth cadence in the 80-to-90–rpm range, and this is accomplished by making slight adjustments frequently.

For more information on cycling technique, consult one of the specialty books listed in the appendix.

SWIMMING

*M*y approach to swimming is that you should be able to swim well and fast enough to ensure that you'll be psychologically comfortable and safe in the water. When I started out, I rotated strokes between crawl, sidestroke, and backstroke. (Rather than the Australian crawl or freestyle, which uses the flutter kick, I do a stroke called the "trudgeon crawl." It combines the crawl arm stroke with a frog kick. It's an uncommon stroke that I happen to be most comfortable with.)

In the races I generally do just the trudgeon crawl. But if you want to sidestroke, breaststroke, or even backstroke, either the whole way or part of it, while alternating with the crawl, that's fine. Whatever works for you. If you're going to have a really slow swim, you must only be sure that you can go fast enough to beat the swim cutoff time (if there is one).

As long as you feel *psychologically* comfortable in the water, swimming is a *physically* comfortable sport. The water supports most of your weight while you're swimming. There's none of the pounding, twisting, and jarring associated with running. Although swimming is mainly an upper-body sport, your lower body does get some work, especially if you use the breaststroke or sidestroke or trudgeon crawl, with a frog or scissors kick. Assuming that you know how to swim and adhere to proper water-safety rules wherever you're swimming, it's a safe sport, with a fairly low level of intrinsic-injury risk.

There can be problems connected with finding a suitable place for your swim training. Most triathlon swims are in open water. Thus, doing your swim training in open water is ideal. Further, open-water swimming in a lake or a body of salt water provides a feeling of freedom seldom found in the other regular-exercise sports. And there are no pool schedules to stick to.

However, this kind of swimming has its own problems: accessibility and availability, suitable water conditions and temperature, safety considerations (e.g., the possible presence of boats under way to look out for, the possible absence of lifeguards should you get into trouble), the necessity of using a wetsuit every time if the water you're swimming in is cold. Otherwise, you'll be using a pool at a health club, "Y," or educational facility with public hours for the pool. That may require doing your swim workouts on a schedule, and/or sharing swim-lap lanes in the pool with others (which is easy to get used to, by the way).

As noted, good swimming technique is somewhat complex and takes some time and practice to learn. In my view, without hands-on instruction few people can learn to swim safely and efficiently on their own. If you don't know how to swim but want to try it, find a local "Y" or swim club that offers lessons. It's very easy to get into bad swim-technique habits without knowing it. For many, there's a certain amount of fear to overcome. Personal instruction can really help in dealing with these problems as well as with the technical aspects of the sport. As noted, while it's tough to learn how to swim from scratch using a book, if you've already done some swimming and want to improve, a book can be very helpful. Please consult the appendix.

Smoothness and an even rhythm are absolutely essential in this sport. So is proper breathing, arm position through the stroke, and leg position. So, too, is keeping the upper body quiet beyond the requirements of the stroke itself and the breathing pattern: no flailing of the arms, no extraneous body rotation beyond that necessary for breathing. This will keep the water immediately surrounding you as smooth as possible, thus reducing drag and saving energy. Swimming as horizontally and as high in the water as possible (thus reducing what sailors call "wetted surface") will help you to accomplish the same end.

When in the crawl you turn your head to the side to breathe (most recreational swimmers do it on every other stroke), lift it out of the water just enough to get a clean lungful of air, and then exhale while your face is in the water during the next stroke cycle. Arm-stroke configuration can range from simple to complex. When you're

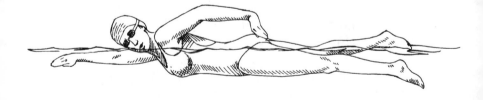

▶ *The crawl.* ◀

starting out to become a long-distance swimmer, do what's comfortable and works for you, as long as you're lifting your arm clear of the water with each stroke and not reaching too far forward for the next hand placement (the equivalent of overstriding in running). If you want to move on to the next level of stroke sophistication and effectiveness, consult a good book on swimming, or—better yet—take some lessons.

WALKING

*I*f you haven't been exercising at all, or have been doing it quite irregularly, and are planning to start out on the Foundation program (see chapter 3), it's a very good idea to spend that first week or two of workouts just walking in an ordinary way, at a pace slightly faster than normal.

When you walk, as your front foot comes down, your rear foot hasn't yet lifted off the ground. That's what differentiates walking from running. In running, you're airborne for at least an instant between steps. That's also what makes walking a less stressful gait than running.

Then, you might wish to move on to what I call "PaceWalking" for the next week or two, before you proceed to running.

PaceWalking

PaceWalking is a form of fast walking using a defined technique that differs from that of ordinary walking. Fast walking goes by a wide variety of names: "exercise walking," "fitness walking," "health walking," "power walking," "aerobic walking," "speed walking," "striding." "PaceWalking" is a term I came up with some years ago when writing a book on walking for exercise (Jonas and Radetsky, 1988). There are two PaceWalking gaits: Exercise PaceWalking and the PaceWalking Race Gait. They're both simple.

EXERCISE PACEWALKING. In Exercise PaceWalking you walk fast with a purposeful stride of medium length. With each step, you land on your heel, feet pointing straight ahead as if you were straddling an imaginary white line, then roll forward along the outside of your foot, and push off with your toes into the next stride. As you push off, you should bend your toes up just about as far as they can go.

As in running, you should stand comfortably straight, but not rigidly so. Your head should be up, shoulders dropped and relaxed. Having your upper body nice and loose makes it easier to develop a smooth, rhythmic, comfortable arm swing. As your speed picks up, you may find it more comfortable to bend forward slightly. Make sure that you're bending from your hips, though, and not your waist. Because it inhibits full movement of your diaphragm, bending from the waist interferes with efficient and effective breathing.

If you want to PaceWalk aerobically, the arm motion is as important as the leg motion, unlike in running. If you're like most people, without a determined and constant, rhythmic swing of your arms you'll find it impossible to walk fast enough to get your heart rate up into your aerobic range. Your arm swing should be forward and back, in the direction you're moving, not across your chest. Doing the latter just interferes with your forward momentum. Your elbows should be comfortably bent. Swinging a straight arm often leads to the pooling of fluid in your hands.

With the forward arm swing, your hand should reach about to upper chest level. On the backswing, you should stop when you feel your back shoulder muscles gently stretching. Your fingers should be closed lightly, your fists never clenched. Finally, your arm swing should follow the lead of your legs, not vice versa.

If you feel comfortable doing it, you can try rotating your hip forward with the forward motion of your same-side leg. This will make your gait look something like that of racewalking (see below). But rotation of the hip is certainly not essential. Don't do it if it doesn't work for you.

At the beginning, you'll probably be doing about 15 to 18 minutes for the mile. (The average pace for ordinary walking is about 20 minutes per mile.) You can get down to 13 to 14 minutes per mile with some practice. A good clip in PaceWalking is 11 to 12 minutes per mile. Should you want to walk faster than that, you'll probably have to learn how to racewalk.

PACEWALKING RACE GAIT. Finally, in walking there's what I call the "PaceWalking Race Gait." Essentially, it's jogging while keeping your rear foot on the ground until you come down on your front foot. Even though it feels like running slowly, you are by definition walking. Your knees are slightly bent through each stride, just as in running, and the arm swing is not at all emphasized.

Your body is relaxed, bent forward slightly at the hips. As with Exercise PaceWalking, you come down on your heel, roll forward along the outside of your foot, and push off with your toes. Your back is straight but not rigidly so, and your shoulders are relaxed. Your head is up, your gaze directed forward. The PaceWalking Race Gait is halfway between Exercise PaceWalking and running, and once you get the hang of it you'll find that you can comfortably maintain a pace of 10 to 11 minutes per mile.

RACEWALKING GAIT. Even with a hip rotation, PaceWalking is different from racewalking, a fine but technically demanding sport. Racewalkers can move very fast, as fast as 7 minutes per mile for over 30 miles in the racewalking marathon (50k). Getting up to that speed requires a complex hip rotation. This hip rotation lengthens the stride without overstretching the leg and enables the attainment of much higher cadences than those of the ordinary walker or the PaceWalker.

Racewalking has strict rules: One foot must always be in contact with the ground, and the knee of the weight-bearing leg must be straight for at least an instant as the body passes over it. This is hard to do without some practice. In racewalking competitions, to make sure that entrants follow the rules, there are judges out on the course.

Racewalking would be a very good gait for the recreational triathlete: fast, but with a significantly lowered foot pressure compared with running. However, I've rarely seen it used in multisport races. If you want to try it, you'll likely need some hands-on instruction to get it right. In many parts of the country there are racewalking clubs from which you should be able to get assistance.

WEIGHT TRAINING

*S*ome multisport athletes also incorporate some sort of weight training into their workout schedule, especially in the winter off-season. I enjoy working with the weights two to three times per week for three to four months during that time of the year. It fits in well when I've cut back my running to perhaps once a week on a nice, cool, crisp day, and my cycling back to two to three 30-minute rides on my indoor trainer with a good book on the reading rack, as well as an occasional foray outside on a crisp, cold day, dressed right for it and on my mountain bike.

Although weight training is ordinarily used for developing musculoskeletal fitness rather than cardiovascular fitness, it can be done aerobically, whether with machines or free weights, and thus can be used to improve the latter as well. It all depends upon the routine you use. Neither power lifters nor bodybuilders generally work out aerobically. Aiming for increased muscle strength and bulk, they're interested in lifting large amounts of weight for each "rep" (repetition) of the exercise in the "set" (the group of reps taken together), but not necessarily in getting their heart rates up into the aerobic range. For them, the key is "high weight, low reps, low sets." They usually take a significant rest between sets, to allow the muscles time to recover.

However, lifting low weight with high reps in multiple sets and taking little downtime between sets can make the workout aerobic. At the same time, muscle flexibility and endurance, as well as strength to a certain extent, will be enhanced.

You can lift weights at home or in a gym. Unless you have a partner at home, for safety reasons lifting with free weights (barbells and dumbbells) should be done only in a gym. And if you haven't lifted free weights before, you should be sure to get some instruction. If while lifting free weights you find yourself unable to support a given load, you might get seriously injured putting the weights down, or worse, dropping them.

Lifting on machines can be safely done on your own. But even with a home machine, before you start you should get some instruction in using it. Training on a group of machines like Nautilus, Keyser, Cybex, or Eagle is necessarily done in a gym, unless you have a lot of money and a lot of space at home.

BREATHING

"*B*reathing," as some experts like to tell us, "is very important." Actually what they mean is *how* you breathe is very important. It's helpful to breathe rhythmically as well as to have a rhythmic gait, stroke, or pedal pattern. When breathing, you inhale oxygen, which is necessary for virtually every bodily function, but especially important to support vigorous exercise. You exhale carbon dioxide, a principal waste product of muscle activity. To get the maximum amount of oxygen in and clear the maximum amount of carbon dioxide out with each breath, you need to breathe deeply on a regular basis.

Deep breathing is accomplished by expanding your lungs outward using your chest and rib cage muscles and expanding them downward using your diaphragm. (The diaphragm is the wide band of tissue that goes across the bottom of the lung cavity horizontally, separating it from the abdominal cavity. Moving it downward enables full lung expansion.) Deep, abdominal ("belly") breathing, fully using your diaphragm, is essential for effective carbon dioxide removal.

As your speed and breathing rate in any of the sports pick up, you'll likely find that rhythmically linking your breathing with your steps or cadence will improve your performance. For example, you might breathe in for three paces, out for three paces. Of course, the right combination for you is the one that works for you.

One exception to the "even, in/out" rhythmic-breathing rule is a routine you can try when feeling suddenly worn out during a training session or a race. Exhale for longer and more forcefully than you inhale, say on a three-count-in/seven-count-out ratio, for two or three cycles. This is very effective in clearing carbon dioxide that has accumulated in the bottom of your lungs because you're not breathing deeply enough.

INJURY

*A*s noted briefly at the beginning of this chapter, athletic injuries can be conveniently grouped into two categories, "intrinsic" and "extrinsic." Intrinsic injury is that which arises internally due to the nature of the sport itself, often from overuse. Extrinsic injury is that caused by a factor outside of the person and not specifically related to the athletic motion of the sport.

Intrinsic Injury

In this group there are, for example: "swimmers' shoulder," which is caused by the unnatural rotary motion of the shoulder that occurs in swimming; "cyclists' knee," usually due to overwork (or undertraining) of the quadriceps muscles in the thigh and the resulting strain on the patellar (knee-cap) tendon; "shinsplints," in running, generally pain on the front of the lower leg, arising from the constant pounding of the sport; dehydration, which can occur during any exercise on a very hot day if you don't drink enough water at regular intervals; hypothermia, which can affect swimmers, especially thin ones, swimming in cold water (for most people "cold" is 67°F or below, but that varies with the person) without wearing a wetsuit. Sometimes cyclists even get "tennis elbow," inflammation of the tendon that is attached to the front of the elbow joint, from the pressure exerted on the forearms during long rides.

Symptoms and signs of most intrinsic injuries (other than those related to heat and cold) include: pain that occurs whenever you exercise and that may well stay with you after you've stopped exercising; redness and/or swelling in a localized area indicating inflammation; and localized tenderness elicited by pressure, even if the pain is not otherwise present. Other indications of possible injury include: stiffness in a joint or in your back; a repetitive, localized noise that's audible when you move; and instability of a joint when it's moved.

You can attempt to manage intrinsic athletic injuries yourself, with the assistance of a good guide like John Hanc's *The Essential Runner* (chapter 5), Dr. Gary Guten's *Play Healthy, Stay Healthy*, or Dr. James Garrick's *Peak Condition* (see the appendix). Or you can consult a health professional.

Some injuries, especially chronic ones such as a common irritation of the fibrous tissue that runs along the sole of the foot—a condition called "plantar fascitis"—can be quirky, however. One health professional can have great success with one group of patients but for some reason or another, not with you. If you consult a health professional and are not getting positive results following one particular treatment regimen, after giving it a good shot, don't hesitate to get a second opinion.

The best preventive measures for intrinsic injuries include: using proper equipment, especially shoes (see the next chapter); starting off slow and easy at the beginning of your training program; not overdoing it at any time during your training program; using a training-program schedule that builds in rest (as does the one in this book);

allowing injuries to heal completely or almost so before testing the injured area again; wearing proper headgear and drinking plenty of water when running, walking, or cycling on hot days; not swimming in water that still feels too cold after you've been in it for two to three minutes or so.

Extrinsic Injury

Among the triathlon sports, extrinsic injuries are most common in cycling. The consequences of bicycle extrinsic injuries from a fall can range from a mild scrape or bruise to broken bones or even death. The latter, although rare, does occur, and occurs much more frequently among riders not wearing helmets than among riders wearing them: in about 85 percent of bicycle-injury–related deaths the rider was not wearing a helmet. Causes of cycling-related extrinsic injury include bad road conditions; drunk or inattentive motor vehicle drivers; wild or uncontrolled animals; walkers, runners, pedestrians, or other cyclists; overhanging tree branches; downed electrical or telephone wires; and mechanical malfunction of the bicycle, among others.

Prevention is the best approach to extrinsic injury, whether for cyclists or for runners (in whom this kind of injury occurs, although less frequently) or for swimmers (in whom this kind of injury is quite infrequent except, for example, in open water where such hazards as boats under way may be encountered). The best preventive measure in the case of extrinsic injury is to pay attention to sights and sounds that can warn of oncoming danger, and attention to the mechanical condition of your bike—all of its parts, including the various nuts and bolts.

When riding you must stay focused on your surroundings. Keep your head up, while regularly scanning the road area directly in front of you, around the next turn ahead, and at your sides. And keep your ears open, too. Listen for the sound of a motor vehicle coming up behind you, or coming along the road that forms the intersection just ahead. When cycling it's an absolute no-no to wear a radio or cassette or CD player with any kind of headphones. The sound is simply too distracting.

When running, using a headset is okay, but only if earphones are the sponge type that you can place in front of your ears, allowing your ear canals access to outside sounds. A headset of the type that plugs into your ears blocks this access and prevents you from hearing sounds that may signal potential danger.

If you do get an extrinsic injury, manage it in the way you'd manage any injury of that particular type, from whatever cause. That would mean, for example, self-management for a minor cut; and consulting a physician for a bone or joint injury accompanied by serious pain, with swelling and redness, indicating a possible fracture.

Getting Back to It

With any injury, one of the concerns is: "When can I get back to training?" While some injuries will interfere with your ability to do one of the triathlon sports, many will allow you to do at least something to maintain both your conditioning and your mood while you heal. Thus, if you've got shinsplints, you can still ride the bike; if you've got swimmer's shoulder, you can still run; and if you've dislocated a shoulder in a fall off your bike (as I did one June many years ago), you can still run while your arm is in a sling.

The most important point on injury? Take care of it before it takes care of you. That is, don't ignore it, and don't let it get you down, either. Remember, one of the really nice aspects of triathloning is that it focuses on cross-training. Thus the risk of extrinsic and intrinsic injury in any of the sports is less than it would be if you were doing that sport exclusively. And, as noted, you often do have the capability to keep going on an exercise program if injury shuts you down in one or even two of your sports.

References

Bailey, C. *The New Fit or Fat*. Boston, MA: Houghton Mifflin, 1991.

Jonas, S. and P. Radetsky. *PaceWalking: The Balanced Way to Aerobic Health*. New York: Crown, 1988.

6

EQUIPMENT

*T*riathlon equipment and clothing come in three flavors: basic/vanilla, advanced/chocolate swirl, and exotic/simply heavenly cherry-ambrosia crunch. In this chapter we'll spend most of our time on the basic, take a look at the advanced, and mention the exotic in passing, here and there. For additional information, especially on the advanced/exotic stuff, you can consult the triathlon magazines or performance-focused books listed in the appendix.

In this chapter, the emphasis is on equipment and clothing for training in the three principal triathlon sports, running, biking, and swimming. We'll go over the specifics of clothing and equipment for the race itself in the next chapter. Obviously, many of the items for training and racing are the same. But there's a variety of logistical matters that come into play in an actual race, which don't concern you when you're training in a single sport on a given day. Those matters, too, will be covered in the next chapter.

Choosing the right equipment and equipping yourself properly is as important as learning good technique, for many of the same reasons. Good equipment makes the sports you're doing more comfortable, more fun, and safer. Being comfortable and enjoying yourself while working out, and avoiding injury, all significantly increase your chances of staying with the program.

At the same time, just as it's not necessary to become overly technique-oriented in order to enjoy multisport racing, it's not necessary to buy top-of-the-line, expensive equipment at the outset (or ever). And unless you decide that a private lap-swimming pool is an absolute necessity, there's only one piece of multisport racing equipment that can get to be truly costly—the bike.

Good equipment, moderately priced, will certainly be sufficient to get you started. Depending upon your attitude, your budget, and what you want to get out of the sport, you may never have to move beyond that level. On the other hand, if you have the money and want to spend it, there will be plenty of time and opportunities to do so later should you become a regular multisport racer.

However, at the outset you may not have to spend very much money at all. You may be able to find just about everything you need right in the "sports stuff" sections of your closet and dresser. Also, you may well find a bike you can start off with out in the garage or in the storage room in your apartment-house basement. The only other important items that you might not have, unless you're already a runner and/or cyclist, are a good pair of running shoes, a bike helmet, a pair of bike shorts, and bike gloves. (Neither of the last two items is an absolute necessity, but with their built-in padding, respectively for bottom and palms, they certainly make cycling more comfortable.)

CLOTHING: GENERAL

You can spend a lot of money on triathlon clothing. But you need not do so. If you can't assemble a basic wardrobe from sports clothing you already own, you can put one together from scratch for $150 to $175 (see Table 6-1), plus the cost of the running shoes, if you don't already own a pair. Obviously, if you're comfortable running and cycling in a T-shirt, you can eliminate the tank top (singlet) and the bike jersey right off the bat.

As a general rule, clothing should be comfortable, and—except for support garments, swimsuits, and wet-suits—loose-fitting. To save time in transition, top-level racers generally forgo socks for both the bike and the run. For the beginner and recreational racer, on the other hand, to help avoid blisters and generally have happier feet it's a very good idea to wear socks. For women, a jog bra is highly recommended. Men should wear support briefs or an athletic supporter.

An increasing number of both men and women are finding that close-fitting but breathable "compression" or liner shorts (they look like bike shorts in profile, but are unpadded) are very comfortable under both running and cycling shorts. Alternatively, some triathletes will run in their bike shorts; and the latter, if made of nylon Lycra, can be worn in the swim, too, if you feel comfort-

TABLE 6-1

Entry-Level Training Wardrobe and Budget

Item	Price
Shorts	$15
Tank top (singlet)	$10
Jog bra (women)	$25
Athletic supporter (men)	$10
Liner shorts	$15
Sweatbands, 2	$ 5
Running socks, 2 pr.	$10
Cycling socks, 2 pr.	$10
Cycling shorts	$30
Cycling jersey	$20
Swimsuit (men)	$15
Swimsuit (women)	$25
Swim goggles	$ 5
Total, men	$145
Total, women	$170

able in them. If you wear them in the swim, don't worry about being damp on the ride—Lycra dries very quickly.

There are modern fabrics, bright colors, and flattering styles available in clothing for both cycling and running, some of it getting to be fairly costly as athletic clothing goes. But when you're starting out, it's best to spend your money just on the necessary stuff at reasonable prices. Then, when you're certain that you're going to stick with the sport—that you really like it—you can wisely spend money on that spiffy-looking, latest-style garment you saw down at the running-shoe, cycling, or sporting-goods store. Now let's turn to some specifics.

RUNNING

Shoes

There are several characteristics shared by good shoes for any sport. First, the shoe must fit well, meaning that it touches your foot in as many places as possible, except over the toes. The "toe box" should be roomy—forward, sideways, and up and down. And your heel should stay firmly down in the heel cup, without sliding vertically within the shoe at the back.

Second, the shoe must be comfortable. Your foot should fit snugly, so that it can't move around inside the shoe and lead to blistering. However, your foot should nowhere be squashed, pinched, or squeezed. Whether you're standing still or moving, the shoe should not cause any kind of muscle or joint pain.

Third, if you're a runner who "overpronates" (that is, rolls your ankle in too far when you land on each step, which is a common problem), you should get shoes specifically designed to resist that motion. Overpronation is a common cause of injury farther up the leg. A knowledgeable running-shoe salesperson will be able to tell you if you're an overpronator.

Running shoes are generally designed to provide good forefoot flexibility, heel cushioning, and heel support. For the heavier runner, there are shoes that provide extra cushioning and support over the whole foot. For the overpronator, more resistive material is built into the shoe along its inside edge, to help prevent the angling inward at the ankle that can be so harmful. There are lighter shoes designed specifically for racing. But unless you're very light yourself, you should use such shoes only when racing. Generally they don't provide the support required for regular training.

If you have a particularly narrow or wide foot, you should get a shoe designed specifically to accommodate it, to avoid either having your foot slosh around inside the shoe or having it pinched or cramped. Some manufacturers, such as New Balance™, supply shoes in varied, labeled widths.

To help prevent injury, it's very important to keep track of shoe wear. It can be tricky to figure out just when your shoe is gone. But it's better to discard a pair of shoes too soon than too late—that is, after you've got the shin-splints or the pulled calf muscle from using an overworn pair of shoes. In the better-quality running shoes, a tell-tale sign of overwear can often be found in the part of the shoe called the "midsole." It runs the length of the shoe between the outsole tread and the bottom of the foot compartment. For comfort, midsole material must be somewhat compressible. As they're used, the midsoles in most running shoes quickly develop little horizontal lines.

Take a look at those lines periodically. Too many of them means that the midsole has become overcompressed. (Just what "too many" is you have to learn from experience with, perhaps, some help from your friendly running-shoe salesperson.) When that happens, the shoe is thrown out of balance. And so is your footstrike, possibly leading to injury, as noted. Also, the wear at the heel of the outside tread is a good indicator of how worn the whole shoe is. If it starts to look run down, have it checked out.

Assuming that you have a good pair of shoes, if you're doing two to three hours of running per week, as a rule of thumb after about three months of wear you should start looking at those midsoles. If there are many lines (or if the shoe appears to be developing a tilt to one side when looked at from the back), it's time at least to pay a visit to the running-shoe store to have them looked over.

Take your time when buying running shoes. Try on a number of different pairs. Walk around the shop in them. Then, when you've narrowed down your choice to two or three, take each pair outside for a test trot, to see if they work for you at least in the short run. If the salesperson won't let you do that, go somewhere else.

Clothing

For running in warm to hot weather, you'll need: a T-shirt or singlet (tank top); running shorts; for women a jog bra and for men an athletic supporter; "compression" or liner shorts, either padded or unpadded, which can be worn by both men and women beneath running and biking shorts in lieu of other undergarments; socks; and running shoes. Also useful are a sweatband and, if you frequently run in direct sunlight, a cap and sunglasses. Also, if you do a lot of running (or cycling, for that matter) in the direct sun, you should use a good sunblock cream on the exposed areas of your skin.

For running in cooler weather, you may want to add a pair of tights, a long-sleeved shirt made of one of the breathable synthetic materials, perhaps a nylon or heavier running suit, a wool cap, gloves, and an ear-covering headband. (For more detail on cold-weather running, see the section near the end of this chapter.)

BICYCLING

Bicycles

While it's indeed possible to spend a great deal of money on a bike, you need not do so in order to enjoy the sport. Beginning at $400 or so you can buy a very nice bike of either the road or mountain variety that will give you many years of pleasure. Formerly called the "ten-speed," the road bike is the one with the narrow tires and the curved handlebars. The "mountain" or "all-terrain" bike (ATB)—in terms of sales in the mid-'90s, much more popular than the road bike—is the one with the tubing, the fatter, often knobby, tires, and the flat handlebars. A third type is a hybrid. This usually has a touring road-bike frame with upright mountain-bike–like handlebars and a tire-width between that of a racing road bike and a mountain bike.

In most tri- and duathlons you can use any type. Don't be shy about using either a mountain bike or a hybrid if you don't have or don't like to ride a road bike. An increasing number of multisport athletes are doing so, and for the less-strong rider they can make those hilly courses much easier. But most mountain bikes are significantly heavier and slower than most decent road bikes. There are a few, mostly cold-weather road-course duathlons that require the use of the "fat-tire" bike, and there is the occasional race like the Team Extreme Triathlon at Wading River, New York, or the Killington, Vermont, triathlon where the bike leg is off-road, necessitating the use of a mountain bike.

There are few official rules governing the kinds of bikes allowed in triathlons and duathlons. The bicycle must be person-powered and be propelled by use of the feet, not the hands. (The use of "recumbent" bikes is prohibited.)

Beyond that, just about any bike that meets the minimal rules will do. I've seen people get out there with an old English-style bike featuring a handlebar-mounted Sturmey-Archer three-speed gearshifter; a touring bike with basket and luggage rack still attached; a local discount–department-store $149-special mountain bike (heavy as lead, but it goes); or that oldie-but-goodie Peugeot ten-speed that's been hanging around the back of the garage since you were in school (or hanging around the back of someone else's garage for years, readily findable through the local classifieds or at a garage sale).

To get started, it doesn't much matter what you're riding on. If you like the sport and have the money, you'll be going shopping for that first racing-dedicated bike soon enough. Before you wander into your neighborhood bike store, there are a few things you should know.

FRAMES. When you go out to buy your first new bike for multisport racing, there are a number of design considerations to bear in mind. The frame should be made of either steel-chromium-molybdenum ("cromoly") or aluminum alloy. Don't buy a bike with a nonalloy steel frame, even if the material is described as "high tensile." The term "high-tensile steel" may sound good, but the bikes made of it are generally rather heavy and not very stiff.

What are called the "seat and head-tube angles" of the frame should be in the 73-to-74–degree range. Lower numbers, found in outright touring bikes, provide a great deal of comfort and load-carrying capacity but limited responsiveness in steering, while bikes with higher numbers can prove hard to control for beginners and even experienced recreational riders.

HANDLING AND RIDE. You want a relatively *light* bike that handles easily and is responsive. It should also be relatively *stiff;* that is, it should transmit the power you're putting into the pedals into the rear, driving wheel, not into flexing the frame, which would waste your effort. Lightness and stiffness are important characteristics of a good bike, whether road or mountain. Of course, you should seek the happy medium in this as in (almost) all things. You don't want a bike that's *too* stiff. It will give you a harsh ride.

Bicycle "fit" is very important—that is, appropriate frame size, proper seat height and forward–aft adjustment, proper length of the crank arms (the rods to which the pedals are attached), proper height and forward–aft adjustment of the handlebars, and so forth. With the guidance of a good book chapter or bicycle-magazine article on the subject and with the assistance of a friend, given a correctly sized frame, you can adjust the fit of your bike yourself. But to this day, I prefer to have a pro in my "pro" bike shop do it for me.

WHEELS AND TIRES. The wheels should be 27 inches or 700cm in diameter. (Those two sizes are very close in measurement, but slightly different, thus requiring different-size tires. Almost all of the better bikes have European-style 700cm tires with what are called "Presta" air valves for the tubes.) To reduce wind resistance, they should have twenty-eight to thirty-two spokes, rather than the usual thirty-six. There are also various kinds of high-tech, expensive wheels, constructed with many fewer spokes, or struts, or a disk. Consider them way down the line, if at all.

Like the frame, the wheels should be made of a metal alloy, usually aluminum. Steel wheels may sound as if they're tough, but they provide a lot of excess rolling resistance, and a good aluminum-alloy wheel will be as tough or tougher. Light wheels require less effort to make them go around. Keep in mind that the weight at the outside of a circle is magnified by the centrifugal force created when the circle revolves. So a relatively small amount of extra weight in the wheel rims can make the bike significantly harder to push.

Unless you become a really good cyclist, you should stick with the standard "clincher" tire with a separate tube inside that can be replaced by a new one (or patched) if flatted. They're much cheaper and less finicky than the all-in-one tube-in-the-tire "tubulars" (also called "sew-ups" after their mode of manufacture) that are faster but only slightly so. When a tubular gets a flat, you have to replace the whole tire/tube combination. Once you know how to do it, changing a flatted tubular is easier and faster than changing a flatted clincher tube, but learning the "once you know how" is not a snap; the replacement tubulars and the glue that holds them onto the rim have to be prepared beforehand, and there is the cost factor.

COST.   You can buy a decent road or mountain bicycle for about $400 (1996 prices). Sometimes a good deal can be found—but you have to ask for it—if your bike shop has a last-year's-leftover model, in the bike you want, in your size. Also, at the end of the season, dealers may get manufacturers' rebates on leftovers of current models. Ask about them, too.

If you can afford to go up to the $750 to $800 range, the difference in the quality of the frame and components is usually worth the money. As for the more expensive bikes ($1,200 and up, way up) with sometimes weird-looking and sometimes conventionally shaped frames made of superlight cromoly steel or aluminum or titanium alloy, or fiberglass, carbon fiber, boralyn, or other exotic material, and state-of-the-art components, wait on buying one of them, even if you can afford it.

First, see if you really like cycling and multisport racing. Second, learn something about serious riding. If you haven't done this, it's difficult to be able to feel, appreciate, and benefit from the features of the more expensive frames and component sets. Finally, regardless of how much money you're spending, it's a good idea to road-test several bikes before you buy. If the bike store you go to demurs on that one, go to another.

COMPONENTS.   Once you get into buying a good bike you'll hear the term "components." It refers to all the bits and pieces attached to the frame that make it into a bike, from the gearshifters and the cogs to the handlebars and the seat. Like automobiles, bicycles are the product of the work of many hands and firms. The frame designer/builder is primary. But he can create a bicycle only by fitting onto the frame components made by a variety of other manufacturers.

You want a bike with the drive train (derailleurs, shifters, chainrings, etc.), the brakes, and the other essential elements (called the "gruppo," simply Italian for "group") coming from one components manufacturer. In that way you can be sure that the elements were designed to work together and will be of quality consistent with the price you're paying. As to all of the other pieces, bicycle manufacturers usually get them from different suppliers; but on the name-brand bikes, they'll generally be of comparable quality.

SHIFTERS AND GEARING.   These days, virtually all cromoly- or aluminum-alloy–frame bikes come with "indexed," click-stop shift mechanisms that make shifting gears much easier and more precise than the old, gradual, "slide and feel" system you may remember from the "ten-speed" you rode as a kid. As to the gearing, don't start off with a "racing cog set" on the rear wheel. Be certain that you have at least one good and low "granny gear" back there to ensure that you'll be able to get up the hills while still on your bike. Rear-wheel cog sets are easy to change, so look into the matter of getting comfortable gearing on your brand-new bike, even if it's a "racing" model. Any reputable pro bike shop will be able to advise you on the proper cog-set selection and on a new bike; if a change is necessary, the store should make it for you at no charge.

SEATS. The "racing" seats with which some of the better road bikes are equipped are generally narrow and hard, but look great. However, they can be very uncomfortable. If the bike you choose is equipped with one of those, don't be afraid to ask for a good-quality but padded seat in exchange. There's a variety of foam- or gel-padded seats on the market that give a very comfortable ride but are still compact enough to provide the control you need for racing. Most decent and better-quality mountain bikes already sport comfortable seats.

HANDLEBARS. Road-bike handlebars are of the conventional "dropped" variety. Most people will find the handlebars that come standard to be comfortable. But handlebars do come in different widths. If you think that you'd be more comfortable with a different spread for your hands, that change can be made. However, since considerable labor is required to make it, it's unlikely that your bike shop will do it at no charge. I wouldn't consider going to a nonstandard handlebar width until I had quite a bit of experience cycling with a standard-width bar.

There's a variety of sophisticated handlebars available for both road and mountain bikes. The "aero-bars" that you see on an increasing number of road bikes at the races are designed to bring your arms in toward the center of the bike, thus significantly decreasing wind resistance. You can get these either as an add-on to the dropped handlebars—called a "clip-on"—or as an all-in-one replacement for them.

At a speed of 20 miles per hour or more, over a 25-mile course, aero-bars can save the rider around 3 minutes. That's nothing to sneeze at. At 20 mph, 3 minutes equals a mile. If you're competitive in your age group, that can easily mean the difference between finishing in the money or out of it. However, at speeds of less than 20 mph, the advantage drops off quickly.

"TRIATHLON BIKES." There's an increasing variety of specialty "triathlon" or "aero" bikes available on the market. Some have conventionally shaped frames made out of conventional (or unconventional) materials but come equipped with all-in-one aero-bars, high-tech wheels, and other assorted goodies. Others have unconventional frames always made out of unconventional materials sporting possibly even higher-tech components.

Even though you might get to own one of these bikes one day if you've got the money and you find that you're fast enough to make use of it, certainly don't make one your first bike, even if you can afford the cost: a minimum of $2,500, more likely $4,000 to $5,000. Learn how to ride first. Then, if you plan to do multisport racing for more than your first season, evaluate your ability and determine the benefits of a tri-bike over a top-quality conventional cromoly- or aluminum-alloy road bike. You can get a really good one for $1,500 to $2,000; add a pair of clip-on aero-bars for $50 to $100, and you'll have plenty of change left over.

BICYCLING SHOES. While the shoe you wear for riding is obviously not the most vital piece of equipment in the sport, it is important. You can use your running shoes for cycling as well. Many people do, especially in duathlons in which they run, then bike, then run again. But a running shoe is not an ideal cycling shoe.

The principal characteristic of the bike shoe is that it has a full-length (road-bike shoe) or partial-length (mountain-bike shoe) rigid sole. Its function is to keep your foot flat during the downstroke on the pedal. If on the downstroke your heel bends down at the ball of your foot, your stroke will be less efficient and you'll lose power. Also, the width and tread design of the running shoe can sometimes make it a bit difficult to slip the shoe in and out of the pedal toe-clip (see next section).

The classic road-bike shoe is that tear-shaped number in black leather that most people can't walk around in without feeling awkward. This is not only because of the full-length stiff sole, but also because the protruding cleat under the ball of your foot tilts you back on your heels. Nevertheless, this is the most comfortable, effective shoe when you're *on* the bike. If you get into serious or even semiserious road-bike riding, you'll eventually get a pair.

In mountain-bike shoes the rigid sole runs from the heel to midarch. This at-least-somewhat flexible sole makes it possible to walk around fairly comfortably. There are mountain-bike shoes designed for use with toe-clips, similar to what used to be called "touring shoes" for road bikes. They have a lateral groove molded into the sole that engages on the rear bar of the pedal. Once the groove is engaged, you tighten the shoe into the toe-clip with a strap (see next section). There are also mountain-bike shoes with quick-release cleats that function like those on road-bike shoes (see next section), but are recessed, to permit walking. The quick-release cleat/pedal systems for mountain bikes and road bikes are generally not compatible with one another.

Whatever shoes you buy for cycling, you should buy your first pair only in a bike shop, from a knowledgeable salesperson.

THE TOE-CLIP ATTACHMENT SYSTEMS. The simplest system is just the pressure of the bottom of your foot on the bike pedal. However, there's a great advantage, especially when you're going uphill, to having your shoed foot strapped or otherwise secured to the pedal so that you can pull up as well as push down with your foot (see chapter 5). (Once you try this system, you'll readily see what I mean.)

There are two ways to make the attachment. One is to have the pedal equipped with the "toe-clip" to which I've been referring. It's a little cage that fits over the top of the pedal. You tighten the cage around your shoe by pulling on its strap. The simplest way to use the toe-clip is to slide a running shoe into it. You can firmly attach your foot to the pedal. But, you don't get the advantages of the stiff bike-shoe sole. However, assuming the tread design doesn't hang up the shoe on the pedal grid, you can get your foot out very quickly by bending down and disengaging the strap's quick-release clasp.

There are now several devices on the market that attach to the pedal, providing an external stiff sole for a running shoe. An increasing number of duathletes are using them to save time in transition from run to bike and back again. The device is making its appearance in the shorter triathlons as well. It, too, must be released by bending down and disengaging whatever system is used to keep your shoe in the device.

The standard toe-clip/pedal system is designed to accommodate the traditional bike shoe. On its sole is a small cleat with a lateral groove in it that grips a narrow transverse bar on the trailing edge of the pedal. As with the touring or running shoe, you put the toe of the shoe into the cage, engage the cleat groove on the bar, and tighten the toe-clip strap. With a cleated bike shoe, the attachment is very secure. But each time you want to get your foot out of the toe-clip—as, for example, when you come to a traffic light or stop sign—you must reach down to the pedal to release the strap. If it sounds to you like this arrangement could be a bit anxiety-provoking, especially when you need to get your foot out quickly, you're right. But technology has come to the rescue.

THE CLIPLESS-PEDAL ATTACHMENT SYSTEM. In the late 1980s, quick-release locking-pedal/cleat systems were developed that make riding with your shoes firmly attached to the pedals much easier and safer. Called "clipless" pedals, they have neither toe-clips nor straps. There are several different systems on the market. In the mid-'90s, the Look™ system was the most common. The Time™ system is popular, too. But in any of them, a specially designed cleat on the bottom of the shoe snaps into or onto a spring-loaded matching clamp that replaces

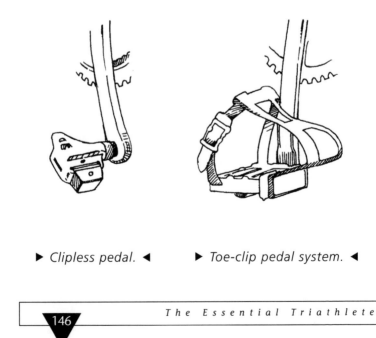

▶ *Clipless pedal.* ◀   ▶ *Toe-clip pedal system.* ◀

the traditional bike pedal. You snap out of it with a simple lateral movement of your foot. Once you become an active multisport racer, more than likely you'll find yourself hooked to your bike via clipless pedals.

Clothing

Bike shorts are generally those tight-fitting black numbers with legs that extend down the thigh to just above the knee. Other colors are available, but basic black is the most commonly used. Bike shorts come with padding in the crotch area. Until recently, the padding was made from the skin of an alpine, goatlike antelope called a "chamois," and the material is itself called "chamois" (pronounced *shammy* in English). Now there's a variety of synthetic materials available to fulfill that function, usually offering more cushioning than plain chamois.

You can wear bike shorts as is, or with liner shorts (which is what I do). If the liner shorts are padded, too, your comfort level will increase. Regardless of what you wear or don't wear with your bike shorts, you want to make sure that there are no seams in the crotch area that could cut into your skin in sensitive places.

Cycling shirts are usually called "jerseys" (the name originally given to a stretchy cloth made from the wool of sheep raised on Jersey in the British Channel Islands). They come in a wide variety of materials and colors. They're not essential for cycling, but they're comfortable, and they almost invariably come equipped with two or three pockets on the back useful for carrying items ranging from your house keys to your lunch.

For wet-, cool-, and cold-weather riding, there's a variety of tights and jackets of various thicknesses and materials available.

Bike gloves have open fingers, with extra padding for the thumb and palm. Providing general cushioning and protection for the nerves in the palm, they're highly recommended for rides of any length at all. The fabrics range from traditional leather with a webbed back to a wide variety of synthetics.

Helmets

The hard-shell helmet is an essential piece of cycling equipment. Eighty-five percent of all bicycle personal-injury–related deaths occur when the cyclist is not wearing a helmet. In the races, you'll be required to wear an approved helmet (see below), with the chin strap fastened. A decent one will cost you $40 to $50, although you can spend up to $120 for a top-of-the-line model. Two important design characteristics to take into account when choosing a helmet—other than fit and comfort, of course—are coolness and weight. Generally, the cooler and lighter the helmet is (while still meeting the safety standards), the more expensive it will be.

Only helmets that are certified by the Snell Memorial Foundation ("Snell"), the American National Standards Institute ("ANSI"), or the American Society for Testing Materials ("ASTM") (or by a combination of these agencies) are approved for use in any organized multisport race that I'm aware of. (If you find a triathlon or duathlon that does not require the use of a certified helmet, don't enter that race. It's likely that the safety standards of such a venue are low all around.) Certification is indicated by the presence of the certifying agency's sticker on the helmet headliner.

Snell is the only organization that actually tests the helmets it certifies for crashworthiness and protective capability. It tests new helmet models when they're introduced and then, over time, purchases random samples off the shelf and tests them again. ANSI and ASTM are industry-supported groups that set standards to be voluntarily met by the helmet manufacturers. The presence of an ANSI or ASTM sticker indicates that the helmet manufacturer has certified that it has met the established standards.

As to proper fit, it's important to make sure that the ear straps on the helmet are properly adjusted so that it can't slip off your head should you fall; that you wear the helmet down over your forehead, sitting just above the tops of your ears, and not perched on the top or back of your head, where it may be cool, but can do you little good in a fall; and that the chin strap is adjusted as tightly as comfort allows.

How do you know when you need to buy a new helmet (Bike Nashbar)?

1. You've dropped your present one on a hard surface.

2. You've fallen off your bike and your helmeted head hit the ground.

3. You've left your helmet sitting in the car on a hot, sunny day.

4. Your helmet is three or more years old.

These factors can cause cracks or deterioration in the helmet's foam lining, thereby reducing its protective capabilities.

Other Bike Accessories

GLASSES. If you don't wear prescription glasses, using nonprescription sunglasses, plain or fancy, is a good idea for eye protection when riding.

WATER BOTTLES. Water bottles are made of polyethylene or a similar material and have a closable nipple on the top. You can open the nipple by pulling on it with your teeth, so that you can drink while riding, holding the bottle in one hand. Bike water bottles come in two sizes, regular and large. You'll pick the size depending upon how hot it is along the course, how far you're going, and so forth. I generally use one regular-size water bottle every 10 miles on a warm to hot day. You'll quickly find out what works for you.

Any decent bike comes with the proper attachments—usually two—for carrying a water bottle. These are called "cages." If you're going to ride for any distance at all (more than 30 minutes), it's a good idea to carry at least one water bottle. With the wind in your face, it's easy to become dehydrated on a bike, even when it's not very hot. And you should get into the habit of drinking regularly, before you get thirsty.

COMPUTERS. There's a variety of small bike computers that will tell you your speed, distance, elapsed time, and in some cases cadence (pedal revolutions per minute), as well as other less important pieces of data. The information that the computer needs in order to make its calculations is passed to it by one or more sensors fitted to either the front or back wheel and to the corresponding fork. The sensors may be connected to the computer by wire (the most common arrangement) or remotely, using weak radio waves. There are also computers that have an electronic heart-rate monitor built in, at added cost. Computers are generally priced in the $25 to $100 range.

REPAIR KIT AND TOOLS. You should carry a portable air pump that can be stowed on the bike frame, as well as a spare tube and/or patch kit. Should you happen to get a flat on the road, you'd then be able to fix it. You can learn how to change a flat bike-tire tube by reading about it, but there's nothing like a hands-on lesson from your local bike-store mechanic. (Ask about that before you buy a bike. If the salesperson demurs, think about shopping elsewhere.) Unless you're into really high performance cycling, you should look into installing "kevlar-belted" tires. They may cost a bit more, but they're highly flat-resistant. You might also want to consider carrying a small CO_2 cylinder for instant inflation of a tube newly installed on the road.

The spare tube, patch kit, miniature "tire irons" you'll need to change a flat, CO_2 cylinder, and a useful multipurpose folding bike tool can be carried in a neat pouch designed to fit under the bike seat.

You'll most likely also want to have a floor-model air pump at home, with a pressure gauge attached. It's important to keep your tires fully inflated—pumped to the recommended pressure you can usually find in a message printed on the side-tire casing—at least for every other ride. Among other things, this will prevent the "pinch flats" that occur when an underinflated tire hits a bump and a small piece of the tube gets caught under the inside rim of the wheel as it flexes.

All of these accessories, from tools to a modest computer, can be purchased together in a package for about $175, including installation of the computer, although you can install that yourself, with a little patience.

Bike-Transport Equipment

BIKE RACKS. If you're driving to a race, you'll need either a vehicle roomy enough to hold your bike (and some people manage to shoehorn bikes into very small spaces in cars), or a bike rack. Bike racks are available both for the car roof and for its rear (mounted on the trunk of a sedan or the towing attachment of a sport-utility vehicle or station wagon). A good roof rack provides a more secure ride for your bike(s) but will run $200 and up, and it will need to be installed permanently (at least for the season). (Many of them can be adapted to other uses, however, such as carrying skis or surfboards.) Rear-mounted racks are less expensive, in the $75 to $150 range, and can be put on your car and taken off each time you travel to a race.

BIKE CARRYING CASES. If you're flying to a race, you'll need an airplane carrying case for your bike. From experience, I recommend only a hard-sided one. You'll have to be able to dismantle and reassemble your bike to at least some extent to pack it into one of these boxes. The big difference among them is whether rear-wheel dismounting is required or not. I found a case that doesn't require it, with which I'm very happy. Hard-sided cases cost $300 and up.

INDOOR TRAINERS. You can ride your bike year-round. If you're properly dressed, you can have great fun riding outdoors on a clear, crisp winter day when the roads are dry. But with an indoor trainer, you can continue to ride your bike regardless of weather and road conditions.

There are two types of indoor-training mechanisms. With the first, riding indoors is accomplished by mounting your road bike on a device called an "indoor trainer." The important features of this device are that it clamps the bike firmly in place and provides a smooth, adjustable resistance when you pedal. In addition, you can vary the resistance by changing gears on your bike as you ride.

A good indoor trainer costs $125 to $150. If you already own a road bike and want to ride indoors in the winter, a trainer is obviously the cheapest solution (rather than buying an exercise bike). You just bring in your bike and mount it securely on the trainer, and you're ready to ride. One fun way to ride indoors is to set up your bike in front of a television set or equip it with a reading stand. However, if you do either one, you have to remember to keep your cadence up while pedaling or you won't get too much benefit from your workout.

The second option for indoor riding is "rollers." Rollers are to cyclists what treadmills are to runners. The device consists of two pairs of rotating tubes that are mounted on a frame. With the front and back bike wheels positioned on the rollers, you ride as if you were out on the road. However, rollers are more difficult to use and definitely not recommended for beginners.

SWIM STUFF

Suits

Assembling your swim stuff is a fairly straightforward task. At the minimum, you need only a swimsuit, goggles, and a cap (for those occasional races that don't supply one—most do; check the race directions). The swimsuit should be made of Lycra or a similar close-fitting fabric. Men should not wear boxer-style suits; they just create drag.

Because most races don't provide changing tents (except the long ones) and a rule prohibits completely disrobing in the transition area, most triathletes wear their swimsuits throughout the race, regardless of what they may put over them for the bike leg and/or the run. Racers who want to go fast and not use up time in the transitions just wear their swimsuits, period. And "triathlon" bathing suits for both men and women are now available with crotch pads that offer a bit of comfort on the bike—but not much.

So, if you're not worried too much about time, it will be a good idea to slip on a pair of bike shorts over your swimsuit for that leg. And if you want to avoid upper-thigh chafing, it will be a good idea to slip on a pair of running shorts for that segment of the race. Alternatively, if you wear a wetsuit for the swim, as I do, you can wear your bike liner-shorts under it in the water (the shorts will dry out quickly enough once you're under way on the bike) and put your bike shorts and then your running shorts over them. Or, for men, when not wearing a wetsuit you can wear liner shorts under your bathing suit and in the swim–bike transition just slip your bathing suit off and your bike shorts on. Finally, as previously noted, you can simply wear your bike shorts for the whole race. Obviously, there are many choices!

Goggles

Most triathletes wear the classic small, close-fitting racing goggles that cover just the eyes. I always found the standard, inexpensive ones to be rather uncomfortable. There are some newer eyes-only designs, which for a bit more money can provide you with considerably more comfort.

I had always swum with a nose clip, until some years ago when I switched over from standard swim goggles to a dive goggle (not a full mask) that covers my nose as well as my eyes and has a very comfortable rubberized rim all the way around. I'm sure that this goggle creates some measurable excess drag, but then, I'm not swimming for speed.

A few extras are: antifog solution for your goggles (recommended), earplugs if you need them (I do), and swim shoes for comfortably making your way from the transition area to the swim start/finish and back (highly recommended).

Wetsuits

Finally we come to wetsuits. Most regular triathletes now use them routinely, even when the water isn't cold. They provide not only significant protection against the cold, but also a significant increase in speed through the water by reducing drag-resistance—up to a 5-minute advantage for the mile.

The standard wetsuit material is currently neoprene, a soft rubber filled with tiny air bubbles. There are newer, higher-tech materials coming on the market all the time, but for the recreational triathlete, a standard neoprene suit should do, as long as it's specifically designed for swimming. Dive suits are too heavy and waterskiing suits are too light.

Wetsuits come in three styles: the full-suit, with arms and legs; the sleeveless (with full legs but no arms); and the "quickjohn," covering the torso only, down to mid-thigh. The full-suit provides the most warmth and the most improvement in speed, but you may find it cumbersome.

I started out with a pre–neoprene-era quickjohn suit that I used for a number of years. I switched to a neoprene full-suit, but gave it up fairly quickly because I found it to be too restrictive. I found its sleeves confining, and its full-length legs hampered an effective frog kick. I then went back to a quickjohn, this time in neoprene, which provides more buoyancy than its predecessor. I'm very happy with that choice.

It's highly unlikely that you'll be able to demo a wetsuit. You'll just have to guess what style will work best for you and hope that you guessed right. Correct fit is very important. That generally means it has to feel tight when you put it on dry. Buying in a store can thus be an advantage, because you can at least try the suit on. But most direct-mail wetsuit sellers will work with you to make sure that the suit fits right, even if that means making an exchange. If you're buying by mail, however, do make sure in advance that you can return or exchange an unused suit.

Depending on style, material, and source, wetsuits range in price from $100 to over $300.

PERSONAL ELECTRONICS

Stopwatch

To time your workouts, check your heart rate, and—if you're biking and don't have a computer—count your cadence, it will be very helpful to have a stopwatch. You can buy a good digital watch for $35 to $50. The most important characteristic to look for is that you should *not* be required to have a degree in mechanical engineering to set and use the thing. Also, the buttons that you press to operate the stopwatch function should "fall readily to hand" (or finger), as they liked to say many years ago in the British motor magazines.

You don't need a watch that's waterproof down to a depth of 300 meters below the water's surface. But a modicum of waterproofing is nice, say, to 50 feet. Then, should you get caught out in the rain, or choose to go out in it, you don't have to worry. If you're planning to do any nighttime training (which should be done, if at all, with a partner for the foot sports only, not cycling, and then only if you wear a reflector vest), having a light in your stopwatch would be very helpful.

Heart-Rate Monitor

This is a piece of equipment for the more serious trainer/racer. By indicating what your heart rate is at any time, it tells you just how hard you're working at that time. The heart-rate monitor is attached to a lightweight belt that straps around your chest. The monitor itself consists of a cardiac electrical-impulse–sensing device and a small radio transmitter that sends a signal to a receiver/computer/display unit similar in appearance to a large wristwatch. Some of the more expensive models have a stopwatch built in. (A no-belt system will probably come onto the market at some time in the future.)

Heart-rate monitors come in varying levels of complexity and expense (ranging in price from just under $100 to just under $400). The least expensive tells you solely what your heart rate is. The most expensive provides and stores all kinds of information about your heart rate during a workout and can be connected to a computer for intensive analysis of the data. The manual that comes with the monitor will tell you how to use it.

CLOTHING FOR WINTER WORKOUTS

*F*or cold-weather exercise outdoors, you should wear several layers of light-to-moderate–weight garments rather than one heavier-weight set. Above all, you want clothing that's able to "breathe," that is, let out through the fabric the moisture that accumulates as you get warm and sweat. Old-fashioned, heavy cotton sweats don't breathe or "wick" perspiration in this sense. They trap the moisture in, where it condenses into water and falls onto your skin, making you feel colder, not warmer.

When starting out on a chilly day, you should wear just enough clothing to feel slightly on the chilly side yourself. You're sure to feel hot and uncomfortable well before you finish your workout if you start out feeling toasty warm. No matter how cold it is, once you get going for a bit, you'll begin to perspire.

Polypropylene, Capilene™, or other materials designed to wick moisture are the best ones to wear next to your skin. The most useful outer layer is one made of a "breathable" fabric such as Gore-Tex™, Versatech™, or (at a much lower cost with much the same results) one of the newer nylons. These fabrics have billions of tiny pores that will let moisture out but not let the wind in. A polypropylene layer next to your skin, perhaps another synthetic-fabric shirt, a breathable-fabric outer garment, and a warm hat and gloves can make cycling or running on a bright winter's day that's not too windy very enjoyable. Generally, even when it's not windy, you'll want to wear more layers when cycling than when running because of the self-generated breeze of cycling. And to help keep your feet warm when cycling, a variety of booties is available.

BUDGET

*N*ote to the reader: This is a full equipment budget for the triathlete committed to a regular schedule of races (except that gender-specific items such as jog bras and athletic supporters are excluded). There are two columns of prices, one "low" and one "high." The first assumes that you already own some of the equipment and will be buying good-quality but entry-level items for whatever you don't already own. The second assumes that you'll be buying all of your stuff, spending toward the top end of the price range (except when it comes to the bike, for which prices can go much higher than is indicated here). Obviously, most readers will find they fall somewhere between the two levels. But this table will give you an idea of the range.

Item	Lower price	Higher price
General		
Prerace clothing:		
warm-up suit/sweats	$ 00*	$100
Waterproof stopwatch	$ 25	$ 50
Sunglasses	$ 00*	$ 50
Keys/money pouch	$ 5	$ 10
Fresh clothing for		
after the race	$ 00*	$ 00*
Sunscreen	$ 5	$ 10
Shoehorn	$ 2	$ 2
Equipment bag	$ 00*	$ 75
Swim		
Swimsuit	$ 00*	$ 75
Swim goggles	$ 5	$ 25
Vaseline	$ 3	$ 3
Antifog solution		
for goggles	$ 5	$ 5
Earplugs	$ 5	$ 5
Wetsuit	$100	$350
Swim shoes	$ 25	$ 25
Bike		
Bicycle	$ 00*	$950
Bicycle pump, full-size	$ 25	$ 60
Bicycle pump, frame-fit	$ 20	$ 35
Water bottles, 2	$ 5	$ 10

Item	Lower price	Higher price
Seat bag w/ spare tube and tools	$ 25	$ 50
Computer (installed)	$ 40	$100
Bike shoes	$ 75	$200
Bike gloves	$ 10	$ 40
Helmet	$ 40	$100
Bike jerseys, 2	$ 40	$100
Bike shorts, 2	$ 60	$100
Bike liner shorts, 2	$ 30	$ 40
Bike socks, 2 pr.	$ 10	$ 15
Bike jacket, tights	$100	$175
Bike lock	$ 10	$ 25
Run/PaceWalk		
Running shoes	$ 00*	$100
Running shorts, 2	$ 00*	$ 50
T-shirts, 2	$ 00*	$ 30
Tank top (singlet), 2	$ 20	$ 40
Running socks, 2 pr.	$ 00*	$ 20
Sweatbands, 2	$ 5	$ 10
Cap	$ 00*	$ 15
Wind shell, tights	$ 50	$100
Total	$745	$3150

*Assumes the item is already owned.

WHERE TO BUY

Stores

Choosing the right store is very important when you buy equipment or clothing of any type, whether shoes, bikes, or wetsuits. Generally, it's not a good idea to buy your equipment in a department store. Only rarely will you find knowledgeable salespeople there. As noted many times above, knowledgeable salespeople are critical in helping you select the equipment that's right for you.

The general sporting-goods store, the kind that outfits the local high school football team, or the newer sports-equipment "superstore," may or may not have knowledgeable salespeople when it comes to say, running shoes. Thus you'd best be advised to patronize specialty shops, at least until you know just what you're looking for and need.

The salespeople in the running-shoe store are most likely to be able to give you proper advice on fit and the characteristics of the various models available. They deal with the product every day, and most such stores are staffed by people who, being runners themselves, can speak to you from personal experience and can intelligently interpret for you the comments of other users of a particular shoe.

As for bikes, buy only in a store that specializes in bicycles. You'll be best off in what's called a "pro shop," one staffed with riders and patronized by people who routinely wear hard-shell helmets and black bike shoes. The most expensive bike in the store should sell for at least twice what you're planning to spend. If it does, you know you're in a store where the staff know what they're doing. They have to. Otherwise, they're likely to have on their hands a number of disgruntled customers put on the wrong bikes.

In any kind of sports-equipment store, if you feel that the salesperson really doesn't know what he's talking about, ask to see the manager. If no one is available to talk with you, go somewhere else.

Mail Order

Finally, you can save some money by purchasing from reputable mail-order houses. But, I suggest not buying by mail order until you know quite a bit about your equipment needs and preferences, and about sizes. Since running shoes need to be carefully fitted, I wouldn't buy them by mail order unless you're simply replacing a worn-out pair of a model you've already used and like. I wouldn't advise buying a bicycle by mail order unless you're very familiar with the size, tube angles, and other design characteristics that will make the bike a good one for you. (And then you still have the problem of safe and correct assembly, which some mail-order bike firms can supply for you in certain localities.) And since fit and comfort are important for safety, I wouldn't advise you to buy a helmet by mail order, unless you already know the model and size that work best for you.

The safest mail-order purchases are of clothing. If something doesn't fit or turns out to be not quite the same color shown in the catalog, it can always be returned with ease. Gloves, tools, and accessories like seat bags are also good candidates for mail-order purchase. Items requiring installation are not, unless you're a good mechanic. But if you expect your local pro shop to provide you with the hands-on, immediate service you like, it's a good idea to give them a reasonable amount of business at other times as well, and not just when you have pressing service needs.

REFERENCE

Bike Nashbar. Catalog. Youngstown, OH. (1-800-NASH-BAR)

7

RACE
PLANNING
AND RACING

*T*his chapter is written for both the first-timer and the occasional multisport racer who would like to approach the endeavor in a more organized and productive way. This chapter focuses on triathlon. But it should be helpful to duathletes as well. Even though there's no swim in duathlon, plenty of planning, logistics, and mental work are involved, just as in triathlon.

"GET UP, YOU SLEEPYHEAD"

*T*he alarm goes off at 4:30 A.M. You groggily reach over to turn it off, and just as you're about to roll over and go back to sleep, you remind yourself why it's going off at this ungodly hour, on a Sunday of all days. Today is the day of your first triathlon. Preferably you got to bed early enough last night to give yourself a reasonable number of hours of sleep. But whether you did or not, you do have to get up, *now.*

The race starts at 8:00 A.M. The site is an hour's drive from your home. You've decided, wisely, that for your first race it would be a good idea to get there nice and early, find a conveniently located parking place, check in before a line begins to form at the check-in counter, and have plenty of time to lay out your stuff at the bike rack, attend to nature's necessities, scope out the course a bit—especially the swim, which should be fully in view—and warm up and stretch out.

So, to get there at 6:30, you need to leave the house at 5:30, which is why you set the alarm for 4:30, figuring in an hour to wash and dress, eat breakfast, and load the car with your bike and gear before you leave.

And now, today, you're going to do your first race. You've trained for months. You've completed the necessary planning and logistic preparation up to this point in addition to getting yourself fit physically and mentally for the big day. What follows in this chapter will help ease the anxiety of your first race by walking you through your immediate prerace procedures and the race itself, step by step.

FIRST THINGS FIRST

I strongly recommend that your goal for your first race should be simply to finish, happily and uninjured. Don't worry about speed. Just be concerned about endurance, about crossing that finish line fully in control of yourself, your senses, and your body, without worrying about where you finish in relation to everyone else in the race.

If you like multisport racing, you'll surely be back for more. If you're naturally fast and/or can train up to speed, you'll have plenty of opportunities to show your stuff in the future.

SETTING A TIME GOAL (BEYOND YOUR FIRST RACE)

*O*nce you've done a few races, you can make a projection of what a reasonable finish time would be for you, assuming that you'll give it your best effort. Setting a reasonable time goal for yourself can add some spice to the experience. Set a goal that will take a bit of doing and some discipline in the race, but one that's realistic, that's reasonably achievable. If you make it, you'll feel great. If you don't, and believe me, I don't invariably meet my own projected times, there's always another race. Remember, race performance is the product of natural ability, goal setting, training, race strategy and tactics, discipline, and the course conditions on race day. Not everything falls within your control.

Since I keep a training and racing log (something I recommend), I'll sometimes look at the time I made the previous year for a given race and set out to try to beat it. But more often than not, especially as I get older and slower, I *won't* look at last year's time. I don't want to pressure myself. Often in a race I won't set a time goal until I'm out of the water and on the bike, experiencing how I really feel that day. Then I can make my best estimate of what I'll be able to do in that race if I put my mind to it.

CLOTHING AND EQUIPMENT

*W*ith all the "stuff" involved in multisport racing, it's very easy to forget things. Even though I've been racing since 1983 and I use a checklist of the type I present just below, I still forget things, or bring them along and then leave them back at the car or untouched in my transition-area bag, forgetting to use them. But if you use a checklist, you'll certainly reduce the chance that something will end up in your "forgettery" (as my stepmother Jeanne Erlanger Jonas likes to call it) rather than in your memory.

TABLE 7-1	*The Checklist*
General	
1.	Race directions, registration materials
2.	Maps
3.	USA Triathlon membership card/photo ID
4.	Prerace clothing, warm-up suit/sweats
5.	Shoehorn
6.	Waterproof digital watch

7.	Magic Marker
8.	Glasses, sunglasses
9.	Extra safety pins, one plastic bag
10.	Water pan, towel
11.	Keys/money pouch
12.	Food
13.	Fresh clothing for after the race
14.	Sunscreen

Swim

15.	Swimsuit
16.	Vaseline
17.	Cap
18.	Goggles, antifog solution
19.	Earplugs
20.	Wetsuit, wetsuit bag
21.	Swim shoes

Bike

22.	Bicycle
23.	Bicycle pump, full-size
24.	Bicycle pump, frame-fit
25.	Water bottles
26.	Seat bag with spare tube and tools
27.	Computer
28.	Bike shoes, gloves, helmet
29.	Bike shirt, shorts, liner shorts, socks
30.	Jacket, long-sleeved shirt, tights
31.	Tissues

Run/PaceWalk

| 32. | Singlet/T-shirt, shorts, socks |

33.	Running shoes
34.	Cap, sweatband
35.	Second watch
36.	Wind shell, long-sleeved T-shirt

Here are the reasons behind the checklist.

General

1. *Race directions, registration materials.* Bring along the race directions that come as a part of the printed race application or that will be mailed separately to advance registrants. These directions will (or should) provide you with important information ranging from how to get to the transition area from the nearest town to a brief description of the course. Remember to save the envelope in which your registration confirmation arrives. It will often have your preassigned race number on it. Having that in hand will help facilitate your at-the-race check-in.

2. *Maps.* If the race is in a location that you couldn't find in your sleep if you had to, be sure to take a road map with you. There's no surer way to provoke prerace anxiety than getting lost on your way to it.

3. *USA Triathlon membership card/photo ID.* If the race is sanctioned by the USA Triathlon, you'll be required either to show your membership card or, if you're not a member, to purchase a one-day membership at the race. At many races you'll be asked to show a photo ID when you check in and pick up your race packet. The transfer of race registration to another person is not allowed, for reasons of both liability and fairness.

4. *Prerace clothing and shoes.* Wear whatever you're comfortable with, a warm-up suit, sweats, what have you. But do remember, even in the summertime, unless you're in the middle of a heat spell, it can be cool early in the morning. It's best to be prepared. As for shoes, it's best not to wear your running shoes to the race. Save them for the running leg. I like a comfortable pair of moccasins or old running shoes for pre- and postrace.

5. *Shoehorn.* This simple tool is very helpful for getting into both bike and run shoes quickly.

6. *Waterproof digital watch.* If you don't want to keep track of your own race time(s), this is obviously an item you don't need. I use a watch that records and saves split times, marking off my individual leg and transition times for the record (mine).

7. *Magic Marker.* Only in my thirteenth season did it occur to me that I could skip the prerace line that always *seems* to go on forever (no matter how short it is). That's where a race volunteer puts your race number on your arms and legs with Magic Marker, a procedure required by the race timers at almost every race for easy competitor ID. If you have your own marker, you need only note where the number is to be placed and have it put there by a friend or loved one who's with you, or by a fellow racer at the bike rack.

8. *Glasses, sunglasses.* For those who wear glasses and plan to use prescription sunglasses in the race, as I do, it's a good idea to bring along your regular glasses as well as your sunglasses as backup.

9. *Extra safety pins, one plastic bag.* At the race check-in there will almost invariably be a supply of safety pins available, to be used for attaching your race numbers to your clothing, as required. I also use pins to attach my race number to my bike (see below). But, in the event that race management runs short, or you lose the pins you were given, it's best to pack some extras. The plastic bag is to put your wet swim stuff in.

10. *Towel, water pan.* Bring at least one towel, for drying off a bit after the swim, and for patting down at the end of the race. At races where there's a sandy beach, and where you can't be sure there will be a hose-down available for competitors after they leave the sandy area, having a water pan at your bike will assure you of having clean feet (and no blisters caused by sand) for the bike and the run.

11. *Keys/money pouch.* If you don't have a friend or loved one with you to carry these valuables, it's best not to leave them unattended with the rest of your gear in the transition areas. Instead, carry a set of car keys and your cash in a little pouch clipped onto the waist of your shorts, or your liner shorts, at the small of your back.

12. *Food.* You may want to have a little something just before the race, either real food or an "energy bar" (see page 175, on prerace eating). And while at most races food, often bagels and fruit, is supplied at the end, you never know.

13. *Fresh clothing for after the race.* This can be the same as your prerace clothing, or, if you expect it to be a hot day, it might simply be a clean T-shirt and a pair of shorts. If you wore non–running shoes on your way to the race, you'll be very happy to be able to step back into them now.

14. *Sunscreen.* This is a useful item both before and after the race.

Swim

15. *Swimsuit.* As noted elsewhere, I always wear liner shorts for the whole race. However, if I'm not using a wetsuit in a particular race, for the swim I'll put a swimsuit on over the shorts. Also, as noted, the fast folks will simply wear their swimsuits next to their skin for the whole race, comfortable or not, to save time in transition.

16. *Vaseline.* It's a good idea to apply this stuff to areas of potential chafing, both before the swim and (quickly) before the bike.

17. *Cap.* Swim caps are invariably required, and they're almost always supplied to the racers. For wave starts (see page 180 for definition), the waves will almost invariably be designated by having the swimmers wear different-colored caps, which then must be supplied. However, it's always a good idea to have a spare cap in your kit. Should you arrive at a race and find that a cap is required but not supplied, you won't have to buy one at the check-in table.

18. *Goggles, antifog solution.* Try to arrange time to put solution on your goggles' lenses just before you enter the water. You'll then be able to take advantage of having clear goggles for as long as possible.

19. *Earplugs.* If you use them, as I do, wait to put them in until just before the start. Otherwise you might miss an important announcement.

20. *Wetsuit, wetsuit bag.* Get your wetsuit on, safely zipped up all the way, well before the start. Make sure that it's comfy and that it fits as it should—like a second skin. If you feel warm in it, don't worry. You'll cool off as soon as you hit the water. Make sure that the bag you've brought along to dump your wetsuit in after you finish the swim is big enough to make that dump a quick one.

21. *Swim shoes.* I generally don't wear swim shoes (sometimes called "aqua socks") while swimming because even though they're light and snug, I find them a drag, literally. But if you find yucky bottoms off-putting, and if you expect there to be a yucky bottom at the swim entry/exit, you might consider it, especially if the swim is a short one. But certainly consider using swim shoes or a pair of old moccasins to get from the bike transition area to the swim start and back, especially if it's a long trip or the surface is pebbly or very hard.

If, assuming that the swim course starts and finishes at the same point, you do wear shoes over to the swim start, you'll either need someone to leave them with (and be sure that the rules for the race allow that person to hand them to you when you exit the water), or you'll need to leave them in a safe place where you can find them easily on your own.

Bike

22. *Bicycle*. Has anyone ever arrived at a multisport race without his bike? Rarely, to be sure, but yes. That's why it's on the Checklist.

23. *Bicycle pump, full-size*. It's best to have a pump with a built-in pressure gauge, so that you top off your tires just right, without having to go back and forth from the pump to a separate gauge.

24. *Bicycle pump, frame-fit/CO_2 cartridge*. It's difficult to get racing tires pumped up to the correct pressure with a frame-fit pump. But you must have one with you on the road, for that emergency you hope will never come. I carry a pump even when I bring a cartridge along. You never know if the latter is going to work right or if, heaven forfend, you might get *two* flats.

25. *Water bottles*. As I noted, I consume the contents of one water bottle about every 10 miles in a race. Many races at the Standard distance and higher have water-bottle exchanges at about those intervals. Nevertheless, except in the shorter races, I always carry two water bottles, just in case of emergency. It's a good idea to have a third one at the transition area so you can drink while making the changes.

26. *Seat bag with spare tube and tools*. The bag should be as small and light as possible while still accommodating the essentials.

27. *Computer.* Make sure to put in a fresh battery at the beginning of the season. It's not fun to have your computer go blank just at the beginning of the bike leg, as happened to me once in an ironman-distance race. It's a good idea to put your frame-fit pump, seat bag, and computer in your equipment bag. If you leave them on the bike for the trip to the race they might not still be on the bike when you arrive.

28. *Bike shoes, gloves, helmet.* If you forget your bike shoes, you can always do the ride wearing your running shoes. Bike gloves make for comfort but are certainly not essential. (Those competitors going for speed don't usually spend the time needed to put them on. I do.) However, you won't be allowed to do the race without a helmet. At many races there's at least one plaintive announcement made before the start asking if anyone has an extra helmet to lend to some forgetful person. You don't want to be in that position.

29. *Bike shirt, shorts, liner shorts, socks.* Particularly on a hot day, some racers don't wear a shirt at all. Although in the earlier days of multisport racing entrants were required to wear a race number during the bike leg as well as the run, plus have a number mounted on their bike, many races now eschew that personal number for the bike leg. If wearing a number on the bike leg is required, however, and you don't want to wear a shirt, consider getting a lightweight fabric belt designed for the purpose to which you can attach your number. You can also use the belt during the run and go shirtless in it as well.

Alternatively, for the bike you can wear your run singlet with race number attached. However, I like being comfortable on the ride, so I put on a lightweight bike jersey, as well as padded bike shorts over my liner shorts. But if you're competing for an age-group placing in a well-populated age group, you'll want to wear your swimsuit through the race to reduce your transition time. Fast competitors don't bother with socks either, for the bike or the run. I, naturally, do.

30. *Jacket, long-sleeved shirt, tights.* It's unlikely that you'll be doing long races in cold weather early in your career, but, if you do, make sure not to forget these items.

31. *Tissues.* These are very helpful to have on hand, for example to clean the sweat off your glasses during a long bike ride. I always have them on my list, but almost invariably forget to stick them into the bike-jersey pocket where it would be so nice to have them.

Run/PaceWalk

32. *Singlet/T-shirt, shorts, running socks (optional).* Unless it's really cold, use a singlet, not a T-shirt. You'll be warm from the bike and warm up more on the run. Again, for this leg I pull my bike shorts off and put my running shorts on over my liner shorts, which stay in place. I keep my cycling socks on for the run.

33. *Running shoes.* Again, like the bike, you don't want to forget them. While you can bike in your running shoes, there's no way you can run in your bike shoes.

34. *Cap, sweatband.* I find a cap very helpful for cooling when I run or PaceWalk in direct sunlight. I take the cap off when I'm in the shade, usually alternating it with the sweatband.

35. *Second watch.* Sometimes you may want to be able to time your run independently, without having to make calculations from the time you finish the bike leg. In that case, you'll want to have a second watch that you can put on as you start the run. It will also serve as a backup.

36. *Wind shell, long-sleeved T-shirt.* As with the bike leg, if you do races in cold weather, or do a long race in which you'll possibly be doing the run leg in the cool dark, as I've done several times, you'll want to have some protection.

Eating and Drinking

Everyone has a program to recommend, and the recommendations vary widely (Park, 1994). I've tried a variety of approaches over the years. I go relatively slowly in the races, and therefore am likely burning primarily fat stores for energy (and I have plenty of fat stores to burn). I've found that since this is the case, it doesn't matter too much what I eat the night before, as long as it doesn't leave me feeling overfull and uncomfortable or lead to bowel problems that can be a nuisance on race day.

If you go fast, carbohydrates are important, of course, and you should consider "carbohydrate loading." Consult one of the performance-oriented triathlon publications for advice on that subject. The trial-and-error method will probably be the one you'll use over time to arrive at what works best for you. But for everyone, prerace *hydration* is very important. Start drinking fluids several days before the race to get hydrated up, especially if it's hot. At the same time, try not to overdo it—so you won't have to spend excess time spilling the excess.

As to eating on the morning of the race, there are as many approaches to it as there are to eating in the days just before it. You should eat breakfast, but only through trial and error can you determine what works best for you. In the past, I've used various combinations of fruit juice, fruit, a roll or a sweet bun, and cheese. In my thirteenth season, I switched to two energy bars, with plenty of water, one before leaving the house, and one twenty to thirty minutes before the start of the race. I found that of everything I tried, the energy bars worked best for me in terms of providing fuel and being gentle on the stomach. I suggest staying away from coffee. Caffeine stimulates the kidneys. The important thing is not to *overeat*, giving yourself a full, uncomfortable feeling that can be especially bothersome on the swim.

The Night Before

On the night before the race, it's a good idea to have everything that you'll be wearing to the race set out, and to have the bag(s) with the rest of the stuff that you'll be taking packed and ready to go. In the early days of the sport, triathletes used three plastic bags, with swim, bike, and run stuff carefully separated. Now most people pack one sports-equipment bag with all of the stuff, to make it convenient to carry from the parking area to check-in and the transition area. As you lay out your equipment next to your bike in the transition area, you'll naturally separate it into sport-specific piles.

Arrival

When you arrive at the parking area, unload your bike carefully. If you've removed the front tire for bike-rack mounting, reinstall it, reset the release lever on the front brake, and make sure the wheel is spinning freely.

Pump up your bicycle tires at the car. There's no need to have your floor pump cluttering up your space (and your neighbor's, should it fall over) at the transition area. If you haven't previously set your bike in a lower gear so that you can get started comfortably on the bike leg, do it here.

Racking Your Bike

If you know your race number, say, from a number

on the front of the envelope sent to you with your registration confirmation, you can first go the transition area and rack your bike (that is, assuming bike racks have been provided, which is the case at almost all races). At most races you'll find the racks numbered. You must use the correct one or risk disqualification. A few races do use a "rack-wherever-you-want-to" system. In that case, it's important to note some landmark or bearing so that you can easily find the rack when you come back to it.

Rack the bike with the brake handles on the rack bar. That will keep it nice and steady. Try not to arrive at the last minute, even if you've done many races. Your assigned bike rack will be crowded and you'll have to take whatever space and location are left on it. Last-minute arrival also increases your chances of forgetting something important along the way. You'll lay out your gear on the ground next to your bike and do your equipment changing there.

Checking In

Next, with or without your bike in hand, proceed to the check-in desk(s). Of course, for races that have day-of-the-race registration, if you haven't preregistered you'll go to the registration line. The more popular races generally don't have day-of-the-race registration. I strongly recommend preregistration in any case. You'll avoid what can be a frustrating, anxiety-provoking experience enduring what can seem to be an interminable wait in a long, slow-moving line.

Check-in for preregistrants usually proceeds quite quickly. You'll be given a plastic bag or manila envelope called the "race packet," and at races that provide a souvenir T-shirt, that item as well. Once you have your race packet in hand, proceed (back) to the transition area.

In the Transition Area: Before the Start

My advice for transitioning assumes that you've chosen a one-transition-area race. Some races have the swim–bike and the bike–run transitions in two different locations. That makes the logistics somewhat more complicated (and I won't cover the subject here). The best choice for the first-timer, at least, is a one-transition-area race. You already have enough to think about.

The "transition area" is a flat, open space, usually a paved section of a parking lot convenient to the swim start/finish, where provision is made for keeping your bike. If you want to keep your transition time down, you'll need to plan it out. You could even practice your transitions. I don't do this, and it shows in my high transition times, which drive my wife, Adrienne WeissJonas, crazy; but they help to relax me, and my overall race performance—in terms of comfort as well as time—may benefit from the extra couple of minutes of relative rest. However, that's not to say that you shouldn't work on transitioning if it's important to you.

In the race packet you'll find at a minimum a swim cap (in a race with a wave start to the swim leg [see below], the color indicates to which wave you've been assigned) and race numbers to attach to your singlet and your bike. There may also be a shirt number for use during the bike leg, and a sticker with your number to be attached to your bike helmet. You may, in addition, find assorted "goodies" ranging from a sports nutrition bar to a copy of one of the triathlon publications.

The run-leg race number, which will have a tear-off tab at the bottom to be collected by the timers at the finish, goes on the front of your singlet or T-shirt. If you're required to wear a race number on the bike leg (no longer the case in many races), it goes on the back of the shirt you'll be wearing during that leg. If you plan to use the same shirt for both the bike and the run, attach both numbers to it, one in front and one in back.

There will also be a number for your bike. This is usually printed on an adhesive-backed paper, to be folded over the "top tube" (that's the piece that connects the handlebar stem to the vertical tube on which the seat is mounted, known as the "seat tube") with the two sides stuck together. However, if you carry your frame pump underneath the top tube (the usual location), attaching the number using the adhesive backing could make it difficult to remove the pump should you need to do so. I don't remove the adhesive backing from the bike number. Rather, I fold it over the top tube and the frame pump, and use two or three safety pins to secure it in place. You do have to pin it snugly, however. Otherwise it could slide back along the top tube during your ride.

Arrange your bike gear and run gear in some order that makes sense to you. I usually make a little pile of my bike stuff, on my bike shoes, at the bike's rear wheel, balancing my helmet on the seat. I'll put it on last. I make a similar pile of my run stuff, on my running shoes, toward the front wheel. I put my equipment bag next to the two little piles so that I can dump used items into it easily during the swim–bike and bike–run changes.

Although you don't have to be compulsive about it, it's helpful to develop something of a prerace routine. On the few occasions when I've strayed from mine, I've regretted it. Before my first New York City Marathon back in 1985, I did a stretching routine I hadn't done in months. It included a groin stretch. At mile 6, I pulled a groin muscle, and I eventually had to drop out in considerable pain at mile 17. Just before the start of the Great Floridian Triathlon in 1994, I decided that the water was so warm that I needn't use my wetsuit, even though the suits were permitted. I lost about 10 minutes on the swim and expended more energy in it than I needed to.

Warm-up

The walking back and forth, car to transition area to check-in, will help you to limber up and warm up some. I often don't do any formal warm-up. But you certainly can, and after a few races you'll know if you need to do so. You can jog a bit, for 2 to 10 minutes, in either your race running-shoes or the old pair you wore to the race. You can stretch a bit. You can possibly bike a bit, although few people do that.

The amount of warming up you do will be determined partially by how much extra time you have available. That in turn will be determined by such factors as how long the check-in takes, whether or not you have to use the toilet, and if so, how long the line is. If the race is starting later in the morning than triathlons usually do (7:30 to 8:00 A.M), remember to stay out of the sun.

After I finish whatever warm-up I'll be doing for a particular race, I then put on my swimsuit (over my liner shorts, which I had put on before leaving the house) and/or wetsuit, swim cap, and swim shoes, take goggles and earplugs in hand (as detailed in the notes to the Checklist), and proceed to the swim start.

AND FINALLY, THE RACE ITSELF!

The Swim

Many races have "wave starts," to which I alluded

earlier. That means that the swimmers are sent off in groups, every two to five minutes. The waves are generally organized by either age groups or predicted swim speeds. If there's to be a wave start based on predicted swim speeds, the application form will ask you to provide that information. (You're always requested to give your age on the application form, for age-group assignment.) Wave starts generally make for a more comfortable swim since there are fewer people around you, and they tend to be swimming at a speed somewhat in the neighborhood of yours, so that you won't be climbing over them, nor them over you.

But in your first race, whether you're in wave-start race or not, it's a good idea to start off at the back of the group you're in. This will assure that you won't be climbed over by faster swimmers behind you. And if you find yourself faster than swimmers in front of you, you'll be in control as you go around them. And remember, drafting, or swimming close behind a swimmer in front of you to take advantage of the bubbly, less resistant water he's creating, is legal in the swim. Don't swim so close as to get kicked in the face, however!

It's a good idea to look at the swim course before the race. The course will be marked by buoys in the water. Sighting the buoys from water level when you're swimming is a different matter from sighting them from the elevated vantage point of the beach. So it's good to have a general idea of the course. Listen to the preswim instructions with care. Know for sure which side of the buoys you're to go on. "Leave the buoys to your right" is different from "go to the right of the buoys."

Don't count on following the crowd in the swim. The lead swimmer(s) could always have gotten it wrong. Set your own course to go in the direction marked by the buoys. You should be able to lift your head out of the water while you're swimming to be able to sight the buoys and other swimmers. You should practice this maneuver beforehand. Learn to be able to use landmarks, as well as the buoys. This is especially important on long swim legs, in which the next buoy might be rather far away, and the last buoy in the line to the next turning point may be invisible at water level, even from the middle of the leg.

For saltwater swimming, you may have to deal with tides, currents, chop, and breakers. I've been in races with a current running lateral to the beach where it felt like I was swimming uphill going in one direction and on a water slide going in the other. If the swim is in open ocean and you have to go out through breakers, you should be a strong swimmer and comfortable in those conditions. If there's a wind-driven surface chop, try to time your breathing to correspond with the troughs.

Most importantly, especially the first few times—as long as you're certain that you'll be able to comfortably beat the swim cut-off time (and there usually is one)—don't try to go too fast. (If you think that you might have trouble beating the cut-off time, usually set generously, I should note, think about choosing another race with a shorter swim.) You don't want to get out of breath or cause yourself anxiety in any way on the swim. If you come out of the water feeling good, you'll know that you're going to finish the race.

Swim–Bike Transition

Once again, make sure that you know where your bike is so you can head directly for it once you reenter the transition area. If you're wearing a wetsuit, pull the top part of it down as you trot over to your bike from the swim finish. If you need to bag your suit, bring a bag that's big enough to pop the suit in easily. Towel off, but don't worry about getting completely dry. You'll dry off soon enough in the breeze of the bike ride, and you'll start sweating soon enough after that.

Try to remember to drink some water while you're putting on your shorts, jersey or singlet, socks, shoes, sunglasses, helmet, and gloves. Do not attempt to ride through the transition area. Mount your bike where the race officials have instructed you to do so, not sooner. That could get you disqualified, but more importantly, it could get you or someone else injured.

The Bike

The bike ride is fairly straightforward. Since in most races drafting off (riding in the slipstream of) riders in front of you is not permitted, you're essentially doing a time trial (racing against the clock) with a large group of riders doing the same thing. Don't go out too fast, even though you may be very excited about having exited the water feeling good. Don't worry about passing or being passed. Get comfortable. Find your pace. Ride your own race.

Remember to drink from your water bottles. That's what they're there for. If you wait to drink until you're feeling dry, you've waited too long and won't be able to catch up at any point during the race. That's simply the way our bodies work. By the way, you might want to fill your water bottles with something other than water. There's a variety of sports drinks in powdered and liquid form on the market, as you know. Trial and error will tell you if one of them works better for you than plain water does. I prefer plain water.

If you've had a chance to go over the course before the race, you'll know if there are any significant hills, and where they are. Make sure that you get down into a low enough gear to make any hill comfortably, before you start ascending. It can be tough downshifting on a fairly steep incline. Take it easy on the downhills. The last thing you want to do is spin out and crash. I find that I'm comfortable up to about 35 miles per hour on a long downhill. (Fast riders will get up to 60!) Anything over that and I'll start braking a bit.

When you get to the last mile or two of the bike, start easing up a bit. Don't hammer all the way in. Drop your gear down a notch or two lower than you'd usually set it for that terrain, so that you can pedal easily. You'll soon be finding out about the difficulties in making the bike-to-run changeover. Many find that spinning at a higher cadence than your usual one for the last quarter to half mile is very helpful.

Bike–Run Transition

Dismount where you're told to. Make sure you know where your bike was before you left, so that you won't have to waste time wandering around the transition area looking for your pile of stuff. Take a drink while you're changing your clothing, either from the water bottle you set aside for that purpose, or from one still on the bike with water in it. Walk or at most jog gently through the transition area to the run start. If you're anything like most of the rest of us, you'll find your legs feeling either very wobbly or very stiff under you. That's why, by the way, it's a good idea to do a few "bricks" (bike/run workouts) during your training. You'll have some idea of what's coming.

The Run

The main thing about the run is getting started. Finishing it will take care of itself. But, oh, do your legs feel funny. You've just come off 30 to 120 minutes of heavy use of your front thigh muscles (the quadriceps or "quads") for biking, and you're asking your legs to immediately convert to primarily using the muscles at the backs of your thighs (the "hamstrings"), and your calf muscles, for running. Your hamstrings have been sitting there passively for the most part, and the blood flow in your legs has been going mostly to your quads.

So you need to loosen up your hamstrings and get the blood flowing to them. That usually takes some time. Often it takes me up to 3 miles before I feel comfortable running or even doing the PaceWalking Race Gait. In a Sprint triathlon, that means I'm just getting loose as I cross the finish line! But sometimes I get loose in as little as a mile or so, and that may well be your experience, too. Just go with the flow and don't try to push it, and you'll be all right.

If you're tired or tight during the run and need to walk for a time, that's fine. Don't worry about it. Many people have done it. Remember, the important thing is finishing if you can, and walking is perfectly legal in a triathlon.

The Finish

And that brings us to the finish. Remember to remember it, to savor it, to value it. For you'll finish your first triathlon or duathlon only once in your life. If you've liked the experience of training and racing, you'll surely do it again—and again. But that very first one marks a special time for you, regardless of where you finish in relation to everyone else in the race.

Smile, laugh, shout, jump up and down, dance a celebratory jig, raise both arms above your head in triumph, regardless of your finishing time. And if you haven't come from a racing or athletic background (and more than a few recreational multisport racers have not), be proud—you've achieved something that not too many other people in the world have.

REFERENCE

Park, L. "Smart Racing Tips and Rituals." In *Triathlete*, May 1994, p. 37.

8

IRON
THOUGHTS

The first "ironman" triathlon was held on the island of Oahu, Hawaii, in 1978. Several ambitious endurance athletes, looking for a bigger challenge than simply doing long-distance races in any one sport, decided to string together the distances of the Waikiki Rough Water Swim, which happened to be 2.4 miles long; the Oahu Bike Race, which happened to be 112 miles long; and the Honolulu Marathon, a standard 26.2-mile road race. The combined race started with fifteen men, twelve of whom finished, with no crews, no volunteers, just a do-it-yourself organization and spirit. Within a few years, *the* Ironman had been established as an event on the Big Island of Hawaii, eventually spawning a number of races at the same distances in countries all around the world.

The ironman-distance triathlon mystique is the product of a number of factors, including the televised and widely seen crawling finish by Julie Moss in the February 1982 running of the event in Hawaii—and the television attention that the race has been given every year since. The six wins achieved by Dave Scott in the 1980s followed by Mark Allen's six, overlapped by Paula Newby-Fraser's *seven consecutive* wins, from 1988 to 1994, as well as other factors mentioned, has led to the expansion of ironman-distance racing around the globe.

Another factor that makes the ironman so special is that this is the only sport other than marathoning in which the absolute amateur, the entirely recreational athlete, can get onto the same field of play with the very best in the world and compete—not with them directly by time, but on the same course and in the same conditions. The recreational baseball, football, or basketball player, golfer, or tennis player, can't get out there with Cal Ripkin Jr. or Dan Marino or Patrick Ewing or Jack Nicklaus or Steffi Graff. But the ordinary mortal triathlete can do an ironman-distance race with Greg Welch, Mark Allen, Karen Smyers, and Michellie Jones.

Why do it? Who knows. Because it's there. Because you've never done anything like it. Because training is a good way, a really good way, to get in shape. Because you want to accomplish something that only a tiny fraction of a percent of the world's population has accomplished. Because you want to experience the thrill of crossing that finish line.

Or because after you finish your first, your friends will say to you, You did *what*? Because after you finish your first, people you've never met before will, upon finding out you've done one, say to you, You did *what?* Because you'll grow in the eyes of your kids. Or because you'll grow in your own eyes.

If you're like me, you'll go slowly in the race. If you're like many other first-timers who are faster than me, and perhaps have more time to train, you'll finish with many people behind you. But the point is, if you work at it, and you focus, you will finish, and experience feelings that go beyond even those you felt when you finished your first triathlon of any distance.

I once received a letter from Angie Darly, a Texan who at 16 hours and 55 minutes was the last official finisher in the 1988 Hawaii Ironman. Angie wrote: "I have never been happier in my life." The day after the race she met the top pro Kirsten Hansen on the beach at Kona. "When I told her I was the last official finisher," Angie wrote, "she said, 'Oh, you're Angie! I shook your hand right after you crossed the finish line.' So, like you said, even if you're in the back, you're still important!"

MY IRONMAN EXPERIENCE

I have not yet done *the* Ironman, the one held on the Big Island of Hawaii. But as of 1995 I had started races for the distance five times and finished it three times, twice within the time limit, once well over it. But at the end of each race that I finished and one of the two I didn't, I was both happy and healthy. (And at the one race in which I didn't achieve even an intermediate goal, I still felt physically okay even though disappointed.)

For the first thirteen weeks of each season in which I did one or more ironman-distance races, I went through my regular Standard-distance Triathlon Training program. I followed that with ten to thirteen weeks of seven and a half to ten hours per week on the average, including time spent in races that I did as part of my training program.

What inspired me to do an ironman? I had just finished the Green Mountain Steelman, held in and around Brattleboro, Vermont. It was a stretched version of the half-ironman distance, with semi-inverse order of events: 2.5-mile swim, 13-mile run, 60-mile bike.

Beating the 10-hour time limit was my goal for the race. I was dead last in a small field of eighty-five. I had been in last place since just after the start of the run. I was way behind the next person ahead of me. But I had achieved my goal with a half hour to spare. I broke down and wept for joy.

I was on top of the world. I was tired and sore, but flying at the same time. Two days later, thoughts of doing an ironman crept into my head. I knew that the Cape Cod Endurance was to be held in three weeks. A little voice inside my head said, "You're in the best shape of your life. You may never be in this kind of shape again." At that time I felt that doing an ironman would be the ultimate achievement in triathlon for me. I had already done a marathon in each of the two previous seasons (the Dallas White Rock in 1983 and the Washington, D.C., Marine Corps Marathon in 1984) and planned to do the New York City Marathon that year. (By the way, in my view, marathon experience is helpful but not essential for doing an ironman.) I called the race director of the Cape Cod Endurance Triathlon. "Are there any spaces left?" "Yes. Just send in your check."

I had trained for the Green Mountain Steelman by doing eight weeks of seven hours per week in all three sports, total, after having done thirteen weeks of the

Standard-distance training program the previous spring.

In the three weeks between the Steelman and the Endurance, I did a century bike ride (my first ever), and a couple of 16-to-18–mile runs. I also did some fast walking. I knew that I wasn't going to be able to run the whole marathon leg. I planned to do a run/walk program in it, and needed some practice.

Taking into account the time that I spent actually doing the Steelman as well as training for it and for the 1985 Cape Cod Endurance, I averaged seven and a half hours per week over an eleven-week period. I usually worked out five days per week, sometimes six, never seven. I did two workouts on about half of those days. Thus, without doing an overwhelming amount of training, I successfully completed the race, and felt great at the end.

The key to success in an ironman-distance race for any recreational triathlete is *setting a reasonable goal for yourself*, in relation to your true capabilities for speed. Let's say that you're inherently slow, like me, but fast enough to have a reasonable chance to make the distances within the time limit: Simply set as your goal for your first ironman-distance race finishing within the time limit.

I knew that my goal for the ironman, of finishing within the time limit of 17 hours, was a realistic one for me. I knew how fast I could swim a mile, and was confident that I could stay in the water for the hour and a half plus I estimated it would take me to swim the distance. I knew how many miles per hour I could expect to average over the 112-mile bike leg. And I knew what my previous marathon times had been. I then added time for transitions and tacked on extra hours for the last leg, since I'd surely run a marathon more slowly after the exertion of the swim and bike.

And I was right. I did the 2.4-mile swim in precisely 96 minutes. I crossed the finish line for the 112-mile bike segment at exactly 8 hours, even though along the way I took 2-minute rest stops and stopped for that hamburger-and-Coke lunch, which took about 15 minutes. Running/walking the first half and walking most of the second, I did the marathon in 6:22 (nearly 2 hours slower than my personal best in a marathon). I took 20-minute transitions, which provided me with much-needed rest.

After having walked most of the last 15 miles of the marathon leg, I had sprinted the last 200 yards, hearing the *Rocky* theme playing over the finish-line loudspeakers and the accompanying cheers of the crowd of volunteers who were, *mirabile dictu*, waiting for me to arrive.

Three years later I did the Cape Cod Endurance again. This time in training I averaged seven and a half hours per week over thirteen weeks, following thirteen weeks of the Standard-distance training program. I improved my time by 19 minutes (saved mainly in the transitions) and managed to go from a well-recognized last to a thoroughly anonymous sixth-from-last.

In 1990, I tackled the Vineman Triathlon, held in the Sonoma and Napa Valleys of California. I used the same training program that had worked for Cape Cod, twice. Unfortunately, it didn't work for California. I simply did not put in enough time on the bike to handle the constantly rolling hills with any kind of speed at all. (What for Russ Pugh, the race director, was an "easy" bike course was anything but easy for me.)

I learned that not all ironman-distance races are alike, and that the old Cape Cod Endurance was probably the easiest one around. It had no serious hills on either the bike or the run, had plenty of shade on both, was fairly cool, and, being held late in the season, for us slowpokes offered a cool, evening marathon.

Planning is the key word for the ironman. If, like me, you're not particularly fast, come up with honest, reasonable projected race paces for each of the three events. Then you'll be able to figure out, as I did, if you have a reasonable shot at achieving your desired goal, whether that be simply to make the time limit, or to do the thing in, say, under 14 hours.

Times of 100 minutes for the swim, 8 hours for the bike, and 6 hours for the marathon are not particularly fast. And you'd still have an hour to spare in a race with a 17-hour time limit (the allowance for most ironman-distance races).

How Much Training Do You Need?

I did my first two ironman-distance events, when I was ages forty-eight and fifty-one respectively, on seven and a half hours per week for the twelve weeks or so that followed my base training program for the season. After my third ironman experience at the 1990 Vineman, I set out to try the distance again at Martha's Vineyard in 1994, and I upped my training-schedule total to ten hours per week for thirteen weeks (following the thirteen weeks of the base training program with which I had started the season). I also did more hill work and added several more long bike rides. But this was still far short of the twenty hours and up per week that many recommend as the minimum for training for an ironman-distance race.

I didn't finish the 1994 Martha's Vineyard Endurance, dropping out at the 12-mile mark on the marathon. But that was not because of lack of physical conditioning. For a variety of reasons, my head was not in the right place.

Having continued on the same training program, five weeks later I finished the Great Floridian Triathlon held at Clermont, Florida, near Orlando. I was slow, finishing almost 2 hours past the time limit, but my head was there this time and I made it. Was I physically okay? The next afternoon my wife, Adrienne, and I were doing the rounds at Universal Studios!

If you're going for the finish and not for speed, twenty hours of training a week is simply unnecessary, *if you know you can go fast enough to make the time limit.* I swam only once a week, took at least one day a week off, and only in the heaviest weeks did I do two workouts in one day. Some years ago, Larry Kaiser wrote to me that he had done the 1988 Cape Cod Endurance on seven to eight hours per week over three months, just about as much training as I had done for that race. And, being innately much faster then I am, at age thirty-nine he finished 189th out of 400-plus finishers. Not bad for seven to eight hours per week of training!

How to Choose a Suitable Race

*I*t's important to make sure that you know the nature of the course, so that you reduce your chances of encountering any surprises. For example, I doubt that I would ever try the Hawaii Ironman (even if I could get in through the lottery—although you never know!). I don't think that I could manage that endless uphill into the wind in the heat with no shade, on the out leg of the bike to Hawi, and still make the time limit.

Logistics are important, too. If at all possible, choose for your first race one that you can drive to, and one that has only one transition area. If you drive, equipment handling will be much easier and you won't have to worry about disassembling, packing, unpacking, and re-assembling your bike. For the Vineman, a last-minute switch to narrow handlebars on the bike—necessitated by a bike-box packing problem—led to discomfort on the bike and considerable arm pain for the last 50 miles or so of the course. (The pain was gone before I left the transition area for the run.)

If there's only one transition area, you can do the race on your own, although having a crew helps in any lengthy race in which you expect to be out on the course for a long time. (Driving our rented van, Adrienne was with me for the last 7 miles of the marathon at the 1994 Great Floridian, providing water and her gentle cheers long after the course had been officially closed.) With two-transition-area races, having a crew makes life much, much easier. For the one two-transition-area ironman I have done (Vineman, which now has only one), I was on my own. I had to hitch a ride that started at 3:00 A.M. for the 50-mile drive to the swim start from the race-headquarters town where the hotels and race finish were.

If you do start thinking ironman, it's a good idea to do so a season ahead (although, as you know, I made the decision to try my first ironman-distance race only three weeks before the race. But I already had some long-distance training under my belt). That way you'll have plenty of time to plan out both your training and your race logistics. You can find the races listed in all of the major calendars. If you want to get an idea of when they're held, look in this year's calendars. The timing of the major races rarely changes*. While you're at it, you might send for the current year's entry blanks. Then you can get some better idea of what it is you're contemplating doing.

Clearly many recreational triathletes *can* do an ironman-distance race, nice and slow, if they *want* to. They should not be intimidated by those ridiculously demanding training programs we often see in print. The September 1989 issue of *Triathlon Today!* reported that Ken Wiseman did *double* and *triple ironman*-distance races (that's right, there are a few races with double and triple the ironman distances for each of the three events!) on a fourteen-to-fifteen–hours-per-week training program that is in some circles thought to be the minimum required for a Standard-distance triathlon. If you go slowly and train your mind as well as your body, you can do an ironman-distance race quite nicely on ten hours per week, or perhaps even a bit less.

AN IRONMAN-DISTANCE TRAINING PROGRAM, FOR THE RECREATIONAL TRIATHLETE

Doing this program takes commitment and dedication, but it won't turn your life upside down. As with the other Essential Triathlete Training Programs, the

---

*As of the mid-'90s, the ironman-distance races in North America were the Vineman, held in Santa Rosa, CA, in late July; the Ironman Canada, held in Penticton, B.C., in late August; the New England Triathlon Festival, held in Sunapee, NH, in mid-September; and the Great Floridian, held in Clermont, FL, in late October.

Essential Triathlete Ironman-distance Training Program is for the most part laid out in time, not distance. Further, for the most part, you choose which sport(s) you do on which days. I've assigned only the minimum of one swim workout each week, and a number of bricks (bike/run workouts).

The long workouts are scheduled for the weekends, the two-a-days primarily during the week. While there's not the pattern variation among the weeks that you find in the shorter ETTPs, each week is set up with a short/long rotation, and the heavier set of weeks is designed with two off-days. You can use one for "catch-up" for a missed workout, but I'd try to take off at least one day per week. (See the note at the bottom of the training program table about the suggested long rides and runs.)

It's a good idea, too, to add some speed work to your workout sessions. You can use an occasional short session for this (for details, consult the books on triathlon listed on p. 201). The extra conditioning will make you stronger—and strength helps for this race—and it will help increase your margin of error, should you get caught up against the time limit, as I have.

Here is the Essential Triathlete Ironman-distance Training Program. You should precede this with the thirteen weeks of the Standard-distance Triathlete Training Program.

To my mind, the most important thing is to give yourself a fair shot at the ironman-distance. Don't assume you can't do it. Assume you can. Don't focus on your finishing time, just focus on finishing. As I'm fond of saying: "If I can do an ironman-distance triathlon, anyone can."

TABLE 8-1

The Essential Triathlete
Ironman-distance
Training Program

13 weeks at 10 hours per week

Day:	M	T	W	Th	F	S	S	Total	
WEEK			(T I M E S	I N	M I N U T E S)				
1	30	60	90	Off	90	90	120	480	(8)
2	30s	60	90	Off	90	90	120	480	(8)
3	30s	60	90	Off	90	90	120	480	(8)
4	60	30s	90	Off	90	90	120	480	(8)
5	Off	60	60s	60	60	60/60	60/60	480	(8)
6	60s	60/60	60s	60	60	Off	120br	480	(8)
7	Off	90/60	60s	90/60	Off	150br	210*	720	(12)
8	Off	90/60	60s	90/60	Off	150	210br	720	(12)
9	Off	90/60	90s	60/60	Off	150br	210*	720	(12)
10	Off	90/60	60s	90/60	Off	150*	210br	720	(12)
11	Off	90/60	90s	60/60	Off	150br	210*	720	(12)
12	Off	90/60	60s	90/60	Off	150*	210br	720	(12)
13	Off	90/60	90s	60/60	Off	150br	210*	720	(12)
14	The week before the race.				RACE				
	Take it very easy, at your own pace.								

NOTES: "s"= swim. You certainly can do more than one session if you want to. This is the minimum.

"br"= "brick," that is, a bike/run workout. As in the table, eight recommended.

*= The minimum recommended time for this workout. In the course of doing the whole program, I strongly suggest doing at least two 80–100-mile bike rides, and two 15–20-mile runs, regardless of time, if you can work them in.

APPENDIX:
RESOURCES

Triathlon Organizations

NATIONAL

USA Triathlon
   3595 East Fountain Blvd.
   Colorado Springs, CO 80910-1740
   P.O. Box 15820
   Colorado Springs, CO 80935
   Tel. (719) 597-9090
   FAX (719) 597-2121

US Amateur
   275 East Avenue
   Norwalk, CT 06855-9989
   Tel. (203) 866-1984/1-800-872-1994

REGIONAL

There are a number of regional triathlon organizations. An example is the New York Triathlon Club (Box 467, Mt. Marion, NY 12456). You can find the one for your area through the USA Triathlon national office and/or the periodic listings in *Triathlon Times.*

National Periodicals

TRIATHLON

Inside Triathlon, 1830 N. 55th St., Boulder, CO 80301. Tel. (303) 440-0601, subscriptions 1-800-825-8793, FAX (303) 444-6788.

Triathlete, 121 Second St., San Francisco, CA 94105. Tel. (415) 777-6939, subscriptions 1-800-441-1666.

Triathlon Times (the official bimonthly newsletter of USA Triathlon), Box 15820, Colorado Springs, CO 80935. Tel. (719) 597-9090; FAX (719) 597-2121.

220, 220 LLC, 5835 Avenida Encinas, Suite 127, Carlsbad, CA 92008. Tel. (619) 931-1502, subscriptions 1-800-529-9220, FAX (619) 931-1503.

OTHER

Runner's World, Rodale Press, 33 E. Minor St., Emmaus, PA 18098, (610) 967-5171.

Bicycling, Rodale Press, 33 E. Minor St., Emmaus, PA 18098, (610) 967-5171.

The Walking Magazine, Walking, Inc., 9–11 Harcourt St., Boston, MA 02116, (617) 266-3322.

Books

GENERAL

Sleamaker, R. *Serious Training for Serious Athletes.* Champaign, IL: Human Kinetics Publishers, 1989.

Tinley, S. and K. McAlpine. *Scott Tinley's Winning Guide to Sports Endurance.* Emmaus, PA: Rodale Press, 1994.

Van Norman, K. A. *Exercise Programming for Older Adults.* Champaign, IL: Human Kinetics Publishers, 1994.

Yacenda, J. *Fitness Cross-Training.* Champaign, IL: Human Kinetics Publishers, 1995.

TRIATHLONING

Cedaro, R. *Triathlon: Achieving Your Personal Best.* New York: Facts on File, 1993.

Jonas, S. *Triathloning for Ordinary Mortals.* New York: W. W. Norton, 1986.

Tinley, S. and M. Plant. *Scott Tinley's Winning Triathlon.* Chicago, IL: Contemporary Books, 1986.

Town, G. and T. Kearney. *Swim, Bike, Run.* Champaign, IL: Human Kinetics Publishers, 1993.

An excellent "one-stop-shopping" source for books on all aspects of the triathlon experience is the "Velo Catalog," (related to *Inside Triathlon* magazine), Boulder, CO 1-800-234-8356.

RUNNING

Fixx, J. *The Complete Book of Running.* New York: Random House, 1977.

Galloway, Jeff. *Galloway's Book on Running.* Bolinas, CA: Shelter Publications, 1984 (distributed by Random House).

Glover, B. and P. Schuder. *The Competitive Runner's Handbook.* New York: Viking Penguin, 1988.

Brown, R. L. and J. Henderson. *Fitness Running.* Champaign, IL: Human Kinetics Publishers, 1994.

Hanc, J. *The Essential Runner.* New York: Lyons & Burford, 1994.

Lebow, F., G. Averbuch and Friends. *The New York Road Runners Club Complete Book of Running.* New York: Random House, 1992.

Bicycling

Carmichael, C. and E. R. Burke. *Fitness Cycling.* Champaign, IL: Human Kinetics Publishers, 1994.

LeMond, G. and K. Gordis. *Greg LeMond's Complete Book of Bicycling.* New York: Perigee/Putnam, 1990.

Lieb, T. *Everybody's Book of Bicycle Riding.* Emmaus, PA: Rodale Press, 1981.

Phinney, D. and C. Carpenter. *Training for Cycling: The Ultimate Guide to Improved Performance.* New York: Perigee/Putnam, 1992.

Swimming and Water Exercise

Katz, J. *The W.E.T. Workout (R).* New York: Facts on File, 1985.

Katz, J. *Swimming for Total Fitness Updated.* New York: Doubleday/Main St. Press, 1993.

Katz, J. *Water Fitness During Your Pregnancy.* Champaign, IL: Human Kinetics Publishers, 1995.

Tarpinian, S. *The Essential Swimmer.* New York: Lyons & Burford, 1996.

Walking

Balboa, David and Deena Balboa. *Walk for Life.* New York: Perigee/Putnam, 1990.

Jonas, S. and P. Radetsky. *PaceWalking: The Balanced Way to Aerobic Health*. New York: Crown Publishers, 1988.

Meyers, C. *Walking: A Complete Guide to the Complete Exercise*. New York: Random House, 1992.

WEIGHT TRAINING

Baechle, T. R. and B. R. Groves. *Weight Training: Steps to Success*. Champaign, IL: Leisure Press, 1992.

Baechle, T. R. and R. W. Earle. *Fitness Weight Training*. Champaign, IL: Human Kinetics Publishers, 1995.

Gergely, G., S. Aull, H. Newton, and E. L. Knight. *Strength Conditioning for Preventive Medicine*. Lakeland, FL: International Ski College (1035 S. Florida Ave., Lakeland 33806), 1993.

STRETCHING

Anderson, B. and J. Anderson. *Stretching*. New York: Random House, 1980.

ATHLETIC INJURIES

Garrick, J. G. and P. Radetsky. *Peak Condition*. New York: Crown Publishers, 1986.

Guten, G. N. *Play Healthy, Stay Healthy*. Champaign, IL: Leisure Press/Human Kinetics Publishers, 1991.

Resources on Cooking and Eating

NUTRITION, GENERAL

Margen, S. and the Editors of the University of California at Berkeley *Wellness Newsletter*. *The Wellness Encyclopedia of Food and Nutrition*. New York: Health Letter Associates (distributed by Random House), 1992.

The PDR Family Guide to Nutrition and Health. Montvale, NJ: Medical Economics, 1995.

SPORTS NUTRITION

Applegate, L. *Power Foods*. Emmaus, PA: Rodale Press, 1991. Dr. Liz Applegate has an excellent monthly sports nutrition column in *Runner's World*.

Clark, N. *Nancy Clark's Sports Nutrition Guidebook*. Champaign, IL: Leisure Press, 1990. Nancy Clark is a frequent and well-regarded writer on nutrition in many popular and sports periodicals.

HEALTHY COOKING

American Heart Association. *Cookbook*, 5th ed. New York: Times Books/Random House, 1991.

Clark, N. *New York City Marathon Cookbook*. Nashville, TN: Rutledge Hill Press, 1994.

Kreitzman, S. and the Editors of Consumer Reports Books. *Slim Cuisine*. Yonkers, NY: Consumer Reports Books, 1991.

Kreitzman, S. and the Editors of Consumer Reports Books. *Indulgent Desserts*. Yonkers, NY: Consumer Reports Books, 1993.

Piscatella, J. C. *Controlling Your Fat Tooth*. New York: Workman Publishing, 1991.

Spear, R. *Low Fat and Loving It*. New York: Warner Books, 1991.

INDEX

endurance, 24, 57
energy bars, 86–87, 170
equipment, 35–36, 126, 130–133
  budget for, 158–159, 159–160t
  checklist preparation, 166–168t,
    168–174
  for cycling, 136–153
  for running, 134–136
  for swimming, 153–156
  where to buy, 160–162
  for winter workouts, 157–158
Essential Marathoner, The (Hanc), 68
Essential Runner, The (Hanc), 126
Essential Triathlete Training Program
  (ETTP), 14–15, 39, 55–90
exercise, 49, 126, 157
Exercise PaceWalking, 120–122
experience, 34, 51
extrinsic injuries, 106, 110, 127–128
eye protection, 149

families, races and, 102–103
fat, 83, 85
finishing the race, 30–32, 47,
  185–186, 188, 197
finishing times, 28, 33, 47, 191–193
fluids, 45–46, 85–86, 127, 175
flutter kick, 116
focus, 45–46
food. *See* diet
footstrike, 108, 109*illus.*, 110, 135
Foundation Triathlon Training
  Program, 55, 59, 61, 62t, 63–64
Friedberg, Ardy, 21, 56, 68
full-body stretch, 80, 80*illus.*

Galloway, Jeff, 68
Garrick, Dr. James, 126
"Gatorade ironman," 29n
gearshifting, 114–116, 141–142
glasses, 149, 169
Glover, Bob, 69
gloves, 132, 136, 148, 173
goals, 23–24, 33, 49, 51–52, 87–88,
  191
goggles, 154–155, 171
gradual change, 25–26, 56–57
Great Floridian Triathlon, 179, 194,
  195, 196n
Green Mountain Ironman, 190
Green Mountain Steelman, 190–191
"grip shifters," 115
groin stretch, 80, 80*illus.*
Guten, Dr. Gary, 126

half-ironman, 45, 94, 190
"hammering," 94–95

hamstring stretch, 78, 78*illus.*
Hanc, John, 68, 126
Hansen, Kirsten, 189
hard-easy principle, 56, 63, 65
Hawaii Ironman, 22, 29n, 33, 43,
  187, 189, 194
hazards, 45, 71
health, 30, 59–61, 70n, 82–87
heart-rate monitors, 157
heart rates, 70–73, 72t
heatstroke, 47
heavyweight divisions, 42
helmets, 35, 36, 96, 127, 132,
  148–149, 173
Henderson, Joe, 68
hotel/motel accommodations, 97
How to Run Your First Marathon
  (Friedberg), 21, 56, 68
"hybrid" bikes, 35, 137
hydration, 175
hypothermia, 47, 125

indoor trainers (cycling), 152–153
injuries, 47, 50, 92, 106, 108, 114,
  123, 125–129, 134, 148
  books on, 203
Inside Triathlon magazine, 104, 200
insulin, 85, 86
International Olympic Committee,
  12n
International Triathlon Union (ITU),
  12n
intrinsic injuries, 106, 117, 125–127
Ironman Canada, 196n
ironman-distance triathlons, 13, 17,
  24–25, 28, 29n, 45, 94, 187–193
  amount of training required,
    193–194
  choosing a suitable race, 194–196
  training program for, 196–197,
    198t

jerseys, 147
Jog, Run, Race (Henderson), 68
jog bras, 132, 133t, 136
jogging, 107
Jones, Michellie, 188

Kaiser, Larry, 67–68, 194

Law, Joseph, 42
liability, 36, 98
limitations, 23–24
liner shorts, 132, 136, 173
logistics, 45, 195
Lycra (nylon), 132–133, 153